# THE TARGET BOOK OF FUN AND GAMES

*Also available in the Target Humour Series:*

*Fiction*

AGATON SAX AND THE DIAMOND THIEVES

AGATON SAX AND THE SCOTLAND YARD MYSTERY

AGATON SAX AND THE BANK ROBBERS

AGATON SAX AND THE CRIMINAL DOUBLES

TARGET HUMOUR

# THE TARGET BOOK OF FUN AND GAMES

compiled by

NICOLA DAVIES

*a division of*

Universal-Tandem Publishing Co., Ltd.,
14 Gloucester Road, London SW7 4RD

First published in Great Britain by Universal-Tandem Publishing Co., Ltd., 1974

ISBN 0 426 10284 3



*Dedication*

To Chris

Printed in Great Britain by The Anchor Press Ltd., and bound by Wm. Brendon & Son Ltd., both of Tiptree, Essex

# Contents

# Acknowledgements

The Editor is grateful to the following authors, agents and publishers for permission to include copyright material in this compilation: the author, artist, C. R. Milne, Esq., Methuen Children's Books, Ltd., for 'The King's Breakfast' and 'The Four Friends' from 'When we were Very Young' by A. A. Milne, illus. Ernest Shepard; Mrs Mervyn Peake, Peter Owen, Ltd., for 'Aunts and Uncles' and accompanying illustration from 'A Book of Nonsense' by Mervyn Peake; the author, David Highham Associates, Ltd., for 'Old Mrs. Thing-um-e-bob', '"Quack!" said the Billy-Goat', and 'King Foo Foo' from 'Figgie Hobbin' by Charles Causley; the compiler and Samuel French, Ltd., for extracts from 'An Anthology of Tonguetwisters' by Ken Parkin; the author, Universal-Tandem Publishing Co., Ltd., for 'The Hand' from 'A Book of Bits or a Bit of a Book' by Spike Milligan; Daily Mirror Newspapers, Ltd., and Wolfe Publishing, Ltd., for selected cartoons from 'The Bumper Cartoon Book'; the cartoonist, the Merlin Press, Ltd., for selected cartoons from 'Top Sacred' by Hugh Burnett; the author, Universal-Tandem Publishing Co., Ltd., for 'Questions, Quistions and Quostions' from 'The Little Pot Boiler' by Spike Milligan; Messrs. Len Costa, T. J. Coombes, and Cornelius Ryan for miscellaneous jocular contributions.

Please note: the compiler and her publishers have made every effort to trace the owners of copyright material in this book; in the event that any queries arise regarding use of material in this work they will be pleased to make adjustments in future editions of the book.

## Let's start with a giggle . . .

**Tom:** 'My uncle can play the piano by ear.'

**Tim:** 'That's nothing. My dad fiddles with his whiskers.'

What is worse than raining cats and dogs?
*Hailing taxi cabs.*

**Young Man:** 'Good morning, Madam. I've come to repair your door bell.'

**Lady:** 'But you should have come yesterday.'

**Young Man:** 'I did. I rang the bell five times and got no answer.'

When do Red Indians wear buckets on their heads?
*When they become pale faces!*

What goes 99 clonk 99?
*A centipede with a wooden leg.*

The cheapest time to ring your friends is when they're out!

# The Table and the Chair
## by Edward Lear

I

Said the Table to the Chair
'You can hardly be aware,
'How I suffer from the heat,
'And from chilblains on my feet!
'If we took a little walk,
'We might have a little talk!
'Pray let us take the air!'
Said the Table to the Chair.

II

Said the Chair unto the Table,
'Now you *know* we are not able!
'How foolishly you talk,
'When you know we *cannot* walk!'
Said the Table, with a sigh,
'It can do no harm to try,
'I've as many legs as you,
'Why can't we walk on two?'

III

So they both went slowly down,
And walked about the town
With a cheerful bumpy sound,
As they toddled round and round.
And everybody cried,
As they hastened to their side,
'See! the Table and the Chair
'Have come out to take the air!'

## The Table and the Chair

IV

But in going down an alley,
To a castle in a valley,
They completely lost their way,
And wandered all the day,
Till, to see them safely back,
They paid a Ducky-quack,
And a Beetle, and a Mouse,
Who took them to their house.

V

Then they whispered to each other,
'How delightful, little brother!'
'What a lovely walk we've taken.'
'Let us dine on Beans and Bacon!'
So the Ducky and the leetle
Browney-Mousy and the Beetle
Dined, and danced upon their heads
Till they toddled to their beds.

## Some more giggles . . .

**Sally** (watching angler): 'How are the fish today, Mr. Jones?'

**Mr. Jones:** 'I don't know yet, Sally. I've dropped them a line but I've had no reply.'

In Scotland, the local park authorities are employing cows to cut the grass. They call them lawn moo-ers!

Why did the man with one hand cross the road?

*To get to the second-hand shop.*

Two Arabs were in a desert when their camels died. They very soon became hungry after eating all their provisions. Eventually they became so tired that they decided, to save energy, they would go one at a time to look for food.

The first to look was Mohammed El Bahwi. When he returned his friend asked him if he had been able to find anything.

'Well yes and no, good news and bad news,' replied Mohammed.

'All right,' said his friend. 'What's the bad news?'

'We've got sand to eat.'

'And the good news?'

'There's plenty of it.'

**Plumber** (to smart maid): 'Morning, Miss, I'm the plumber. I don't want any cracks about us forgetting anything. I've remembered everything.'

**Maid:** 'Except that you've come to the wrong house.'

# Wordladder Puzzle

See if you can climb to the top of this four-letter wordladder. Start at the bottom and at each step alter one letter. (The word on the bottom rung is HULL.)

Watch your step!

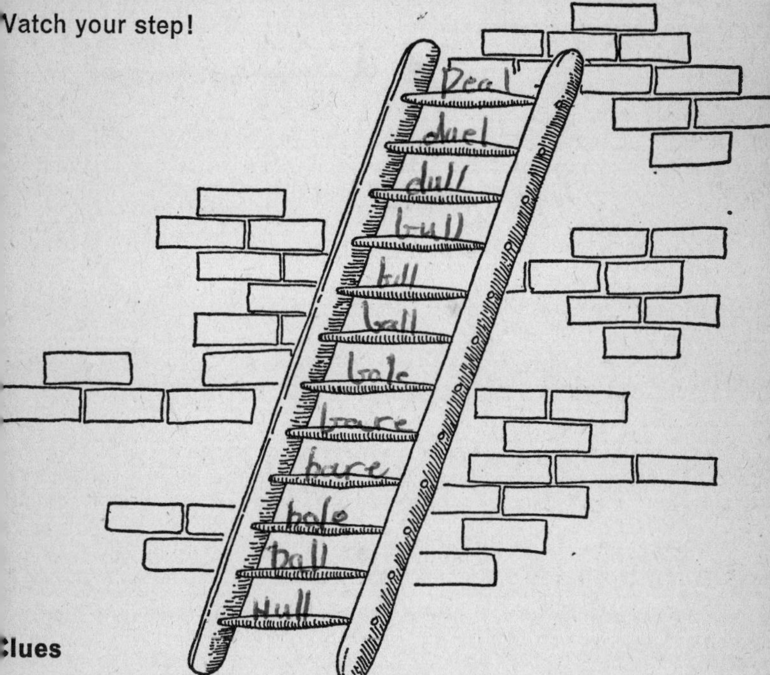

**Clues**

1 Seaport town, the body of a ship.
2 Part of a house, or a large room.
3 Healthy . . . and hearty.
4 March ones are mad.
5 Mrs. Hubbard's cupboard was.
6 A very large bundle.
7 Required in most outdoor games.
8 An account, a boy's name, a beak.
9 A rush makes this animal a reed.
10 If you've climbed up here you can't be this.
11 Trainer aircraft have these sort of controls.
12 A seaport town, a sort of wood, a transaction.

# A Black Story

Two boot blacks, a white boot black and a black boot black, stood together doing nothing.

The white boot black proposed that he should black the boots of the black boot black.

The black boot black was perfectly willing to have his boots blacked by the white boot black.

So the white boot black began to black the boots of the black boot black.

But when the white boot black had blacked one boot of the black boot black, he declined to black the other boot of the black boot black, until the black boot black had blacked both boots of the white boot black.

However, the black boot black refused point blank to black the boots of the white boot black, and said he didn't care whether the white boot black blacked the other boot black or not.

He considered that one boot blacked was enough for a black boot black, and that a black boot black with one boot blacked was better than a white boot black with no boots blacked.

Then the white boot black called the black boot black a black blackguard.

Of course, when the white boot black began blacking the character of the black boot black, the black boot black began blacking the face of the white boot black all black with the blacking on the boot the white boot black had blacked, and the white boot black blacked the black boot black back.

When the Society of Black and White Boot Blackers

considered the matter, they characterised the conduct of both boot blacks as the blackest affair that had ever blackened the pages of boot black history.

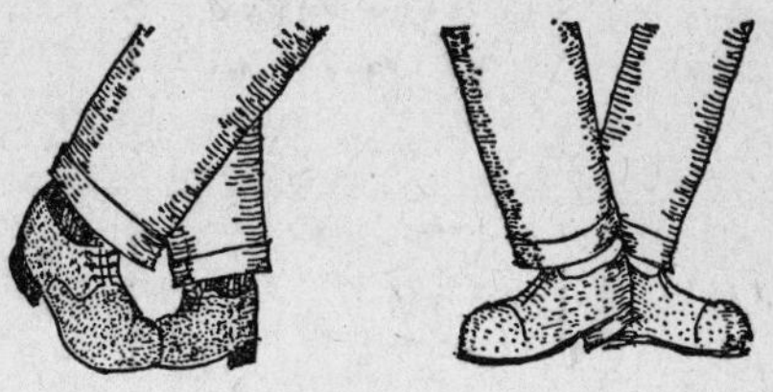

# Simple Silhouettes

## Up the Garden Path

Can you walk round the nine straight paths of this garden without going along the same path twice? The puzzle can only be solved by entering and leaving the two correct gates.

## There was a young . . .

There was a young bard of Japan
Whose limericks never would scan;
  When they said it was so,
  He replied: 'Yes, I know,
But I make a rule of always trying to get just
  as many words into last lines as I
  possibly can.'

There once were two cats of Kilkenny,
Each thought there was one cat too many;
  So they fought and they fit,
  And they scratched and they bit,
Till instead of two cats there weren't any.

There once was a man of Bengal
Who was asked to a Fancy Dress Ball;
  He murmured: 'I'll risk it
  And go as a biscuit!'
But the dog ate him up in the hall.

There was an old man of Blackheath
Who sat on his set of false teeth.
  Said he, with a start,
  'O Lord, bless my heart!
I have bitten myself underneath!'

An epicure, dining at Crewe,
Found quite a large mouse in his stew;
  Said the waiter: 'Don't shout
  And wave it about,
Or the rest will be wanting one, too!'

# Animal Antics

*'That's the last time I give* **you** *dancing lessons!'*

*'It's cruel the way they coop those poor humans up.'*

*'When I bought him you said he was fully grown!'*

# Scholastica Sidesplitticum

'Dad, will you do this sum for me?' asked a small boy who was doing his homework.

'No, my boy,' answered his father. 'It wouldn't be right.'

'Perhaps it wouldn't, Dad, but you might have a try all the same,' came the reply.

**Teacher:** 'Janet, what is the Order of the Bath?'

**Janet:** 'Daddy, Mummy, then me.'

**Schoolmaster:** 'Iceland is as big as Siam. Now, Tommy, are you paying attention? How big is Iceland?'

**Tommy:** 'Please sir, it's as big as you.'

'Mummy, Mummy. All the boys at school called me a girl!'

'Well, what did you do, dear?'

'I hit them with my handbag.'

**Jill:** 'Mummy, teacher kept me in for something I didn't do.'

**Mother:** 'Really, darling. What was it?'

**Jill:** 'My homework.'

'How are you getting on at school, my boy?' asked the anxious father.

'Awfully well, Dad,' replied his son, triumphantly. 'The teacher said that if all the boys were like me he would shut up the school tomorrow. He must think I know a lot, don't you think, Dad?'

# Scholastica Sidesplitticum

*'Hey, Maud!—I've got an "A" for maths!'*

*'And the science teacher said to tell you that a good stiff dose of castor oil ought to do the trick!'*

# How to Discover a Person's Age

Let the person put down the number of the month in which he was born, i.e. January is 1, February 2, March 3, April 4, etc. Double this number, and add 5. Multiply by 50. Add the age the person was last birthday. Subtract 365. Add 115. He must then tell you the numbers that are left as a result of the whole sum. If there are 2 numbers, the last will be the age of the person and the first the month in which he was born. If there are three numbers, the last 2 will be his age and the first will be the month. If there are 4 numbers, the last 2 will be his age, and the first 2 will be the month.

| | |
|---|---|
| Born in July | 7 |
| Multiply by 2 | 14 |
| Add 5 | 19 |
| Multiply by 50 | 950 |
| Add age, e.g. 16 | 966 |
| Subtract 365 | 601 |
| Add 115 | 716 |

Result: July (7) Aged 16.

**Thing No. 1**

NATURE HINT

How to tell the age of a horse:
Saw it in half and count the rings.

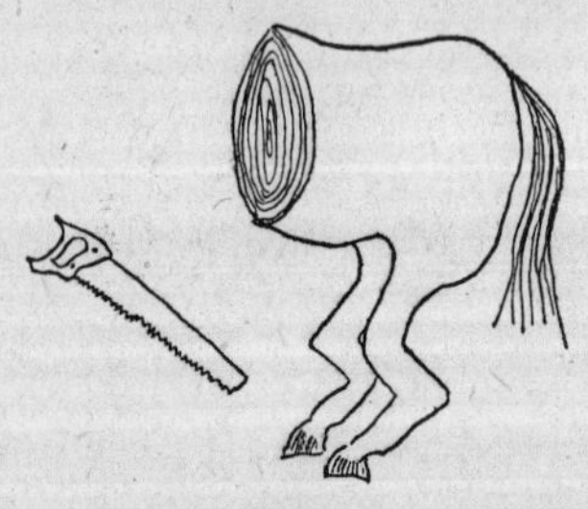

# Puzzle Park

Discover what is in the park by taking the first letter of each object that you see in the squares and building up a word. Some letters are already supplied. (The first line reads BENCH.)

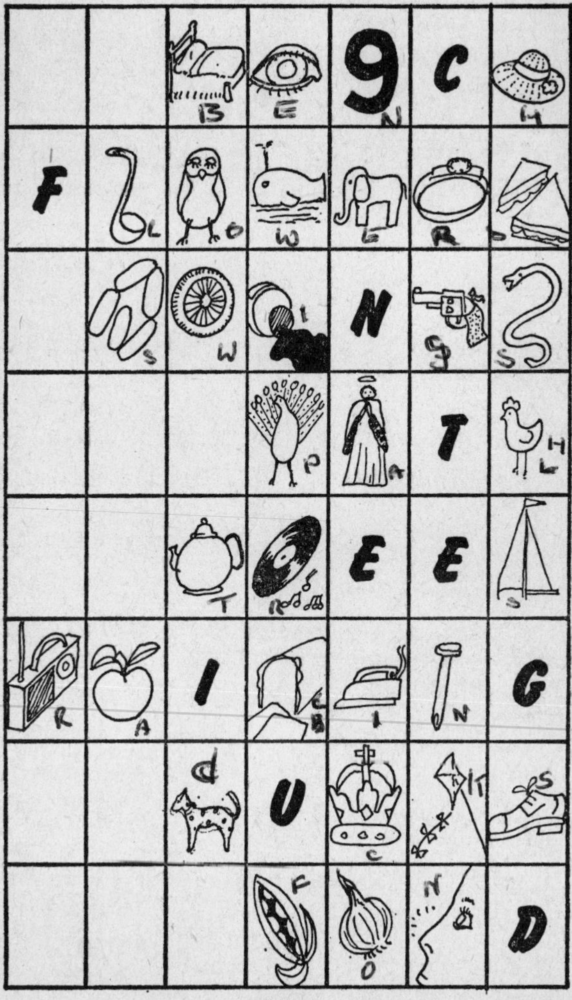

## Riddle Corner

Why is a clock very humble?
*Because its hands are always in front of its face and it is continually running itself down.*

Why do cows like lying on sunny beaches?
*They like tanning their hides.*

Why is a drummer the fastest man in the world?
*Because time beats everything, and a drummer beats time.*

When is an actor not an actor?
*When he is a little hoarse* (*horse*).

Which is the heaviest, a full moon or a half-moon?
*A half-moon because the full one is as light again.*

How high must you hang a man to hang him effectually?
*Two feet off the ground.*

When is a beggar like a happy dog?
*When his tale is moving (tail).*

If you were condemned to suffer torture, but allowed to choose the form, what form would you prefer?
*Chloroform.*

# Nonsense Botany
## by Edward Lear

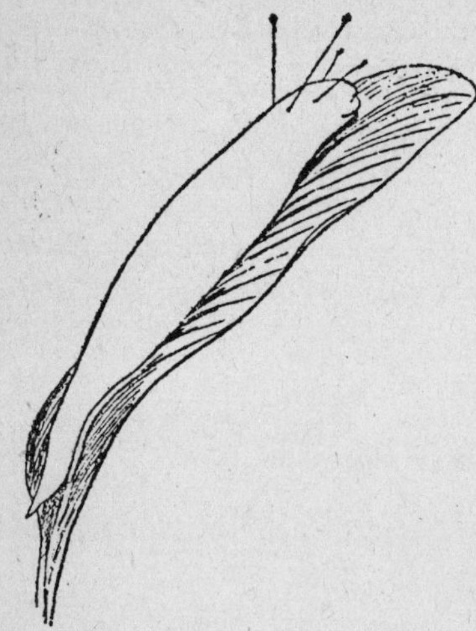

Sophtsluggia Glutinosa

Bottlephorkia Spoonifolia

Barkia Howlaloudia

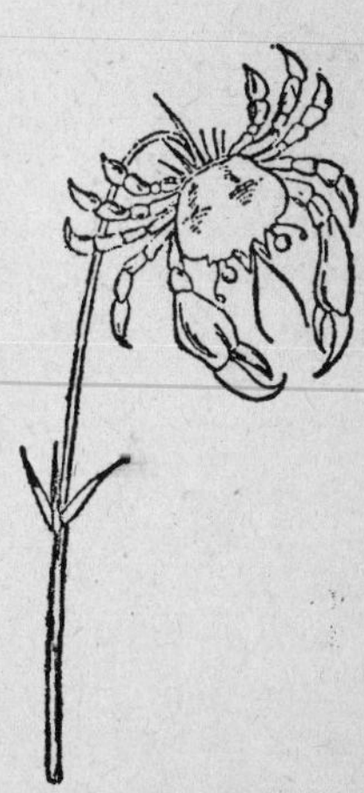

Crabbia Horrida

# Nonsense Botany

Jinglia Tinkettlia

Smalltoothcombia Domestica

Plumbunnia Nutritiosa

Tigerlillia Terribilis

## Grave Humour

Do you know the story about the body-snatchers?

*Well, I won't tell you. You might get carried away.*

Who will be the last man to box Cassius Clay?

*The undertaker.*

Did you hear about the worms that had a meeting in a graveyard?

*It was held in dead Ernest.*

Three dismembered feet make one grave yard.

Excuse me sir, there's a ghost outside!

*Tell him I can't see him at present.*

A graveyard is never deserted.

*You'll always find some body there.*

**Collector:** 'Here, this can't be Cromwell's skull. It's not big enough.'

**Dealer:** 'Ah sir, I forgot to tell you, it's his skull ven he vas a leetle boy.'

Seen as an introduction to a poem:

The following lines were written more than 60 years ago by one who has slept many years in his grave, merely for his own amusement.

**Thing No. 2**

## FIRST AID HINT

What to do in a case like this:

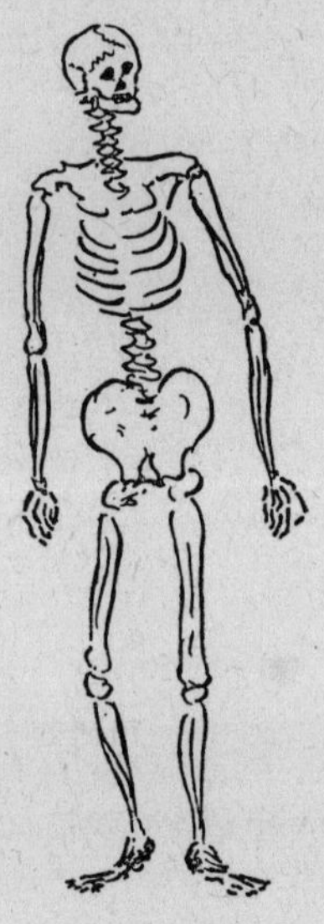

Feed him, stupid!

## Crocodile Tears
## by Mabel M. Stevenson

Beneath the water half-asleep
  Beside the River Nile
Lies, waiting for the bathers there,
  A wily crocodile.

A little Arab boy appears,
  And hastens to the spot.
He thinks it will be grand to bathe
  Upon a day so hot.

The crocodile lifts up his head,
  And heaves a heavy sigh,
And (though you may not think it true)
  A tear is in his eye.

It trickles down his furrowed cheek,
  Says he, 'My little friend,
It makes me very sad to think
  Of your untimely end!'

The little Arab sheds his robe,
  Quite eager for a swim,
That cool inviting water seems
  The very place for him.

But little bright-eyed Selim sees
  That wicked crocodile
And thinks—'There seems to be some risk
  In bathing in the Nile.'

# Crocodile Tears

The little Arab quickly dons
His scanty one-piece suit.
Says he, 'I have no wish to feed
That dreadful, ugly brute!'

He trots off home, glad to escape
The hungry open jaw,
While, by the Nile, that crocodile
Is weeping more and more.

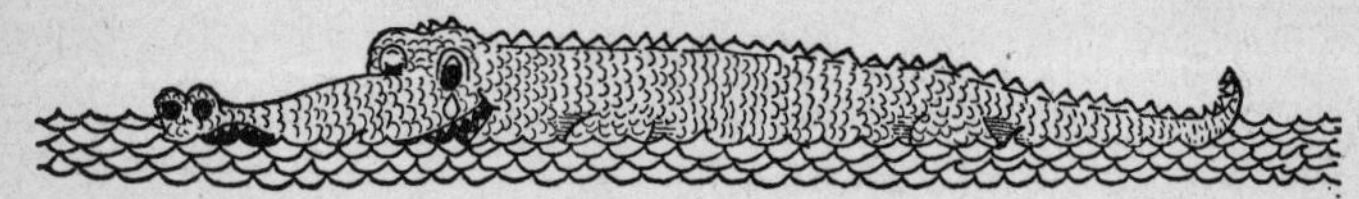

# The Hippopotamus
## by Jack Relatsky

The huge hippopotamus hasn't a hair
on the back of his wrinkly hide;
he carries the bulk of his prominent hulk
rather loosely assembled inside.

The huge hippopotamus lives without care
at a slow philosophical pace,
as he wades in the mud with a thump and a thud
and a permanent grin on his face.

I shoot the Hippopotamus
With bullets made of platinum,
Because if I use leaden ones
His hide is sure to flatten 'em.

*Arthur T. Quiller-Couch*

The lion is a beast to fight:
He leaps along the plain,
And if you run with all your might,
He runs with all his mane.

*Archibald Marshall*

# A Surprise
## by Malcolm Douglas

When the donkey saw the zebra
He began to switch his tail;
'Well, I never!' was his comment—
'Here's a mule that's been to jail!'

# 'Quack!' said the Billy-Goat
## by Charles Causley

'Quack!' said the billy-goat,
  'Oink!' said the hen.
'Miaow!' said the little chick
  Running in the pen.

'Hobble-gobble!' said the dog.
  'Cluck!' said the sow.
'Tu-whit tu-whoo!' the donkey said.
  'Baa!' said the cow.

'Hee-haw!' the turkey cried.
  The duck began to moo.
All at once the sheep went,
  'Cock-a-doodle-doo!'

The owl coughed and cleared his throat
  And he began to bleat.
'Bow-wow!' said the cock
  Swimming in the leat.

'Cheep-cheep!' said the cat
  As she began to fly.
'Farmer's been and laid an egg—
  That's the reason why.'

# Spot the Difference

The pictures beneath are not identical. Can you spot the differences? There are ten.

## A Noisy Puzzle

Add one consonant either at the beginning or at the end of each of these words and make a kind of noise.

For example, add a *t* to hump and it makes thump. (A consonant is any letter of the alphabet except for a, e, i, o and u.)

cream
ban
how
oar
hoop
luck
ail
latter
rash
his

## Jumbled Clothing

Rearrange these jumbled words. They are all articles of clothing, for example tah—hat.

souble
hoess
toca
volges
fracs
krits
sreds
koscs
radacing
ite

## Yet more giggles

What do misers do in cold weather?

*Sit round a candle.*

What do misers do in very cold weather?

*Light it!*

What did the chickens say when they saw their mother lay an orange?

*'Cor, look what Marmalade!'*

What goes Ha Ha Bonk?

*A bloke laughing his head off!*

My brother used to work in a biscuit factory.
He went crackers!

**Sue** (in a plane for the first time): 'Do these planes often crash?'

**Air Hostess:** 'Only once!'

## He Asked For It

'Ticket, sir?' said an inspector at a railway station to a man who had been a season-ticket holder for so long that he believed his face to be so well known that he need not show a ticket.

'My face is my ticket,' replied the passenger, a little annoyed.

'Indeed,' said the inspector, rolling back his sleeves and displaying a powerful fist. 'Well my orders are to punch all tickets passing through this platform.'

## Cave Drawings

*'Of course it's wet. I've only just finished it!'*

*'Go home, Spot.'*

*'There must be a stack of them behind that hill—one drops behind there every night.'*

# Fun with Matches

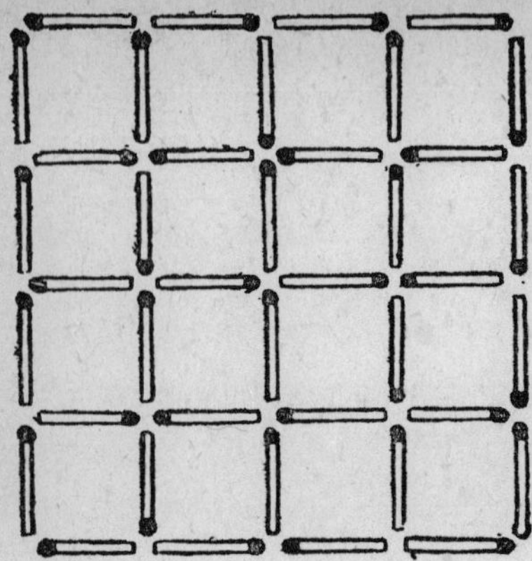

**No. 1**

Remove sixteen matches so as to form two perfect squares of equal size

**No. 2**

Arrange ten matches to form a house instead of two wine glasses

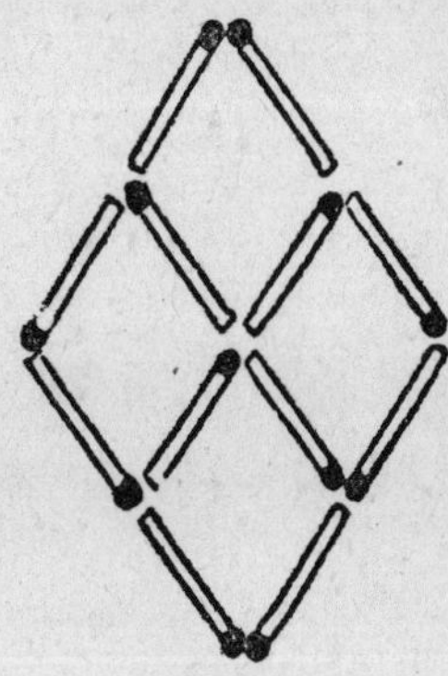

**No. 3**

Out of the matches contained in the above figure, construct six triangles

**No. 4**

Split the bottom of a match and insert the end of another, then lean a third against them to form a tripod, then with another match lift the lot

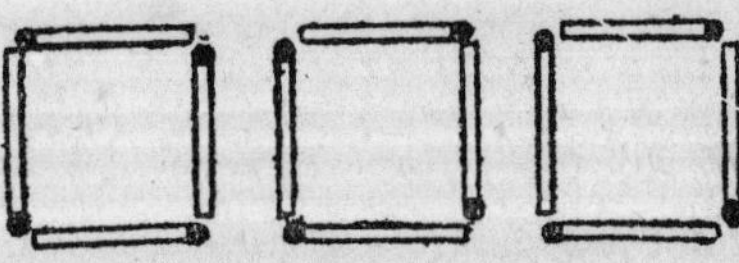

**No. 5**

Form with twelve matches three squares. Take away one, alter position of two, and leave only one

**Thing No. 3**

MORE FIRST AID HINTS:

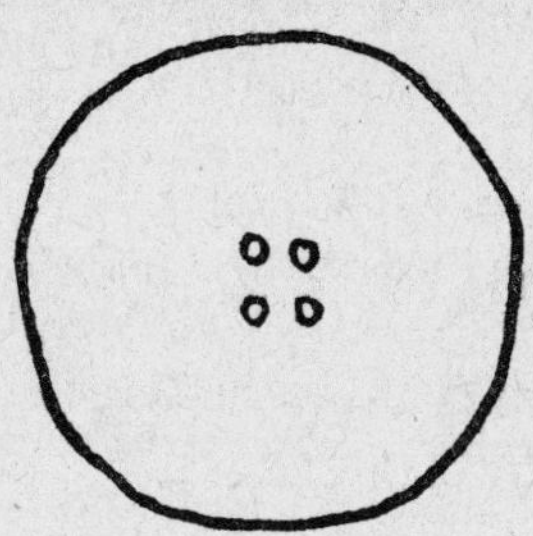

What to do if you get a rain-coat button lodged in your throat:

Nothing. You can still breathe through those four little holes.

Besides, you'll never have to buy another tea-strainer.

**Thing No. 4**

If some poor man faints on the train, take his pulse.

If some rich man faints on the train . . . no, don't take his wallet. That's a *wicked* thought.

## Alphabet Riddles

What is the centre of gravity?
*The letter V.*

Why is B like a clever conjuror?
*Because it can change an ox into a box.*

Why is U the most fortunate letter of the alphabet?
*Because it is always in luck.*

Why is L the dirtiest letter in the alphabet?
*Because it is always in the middle of filth.*

Why is E like the close of day?
*Because it is the beginning of evening.*

Why is C like a first rate cabinet-maker?
*Because it can make chairs out of hairs.*

Why is O the noisiest vowel?
*Because all the rest are* in audible.

Why is F like a cow's tail?
*Because it is the end of beef.*

Why is D like a sailor?
*Because it follows the C (sea).*

# A Fishy Puzzle

**Each fish is made up of letters of the alphabet. Can you work out the name of each fish?**

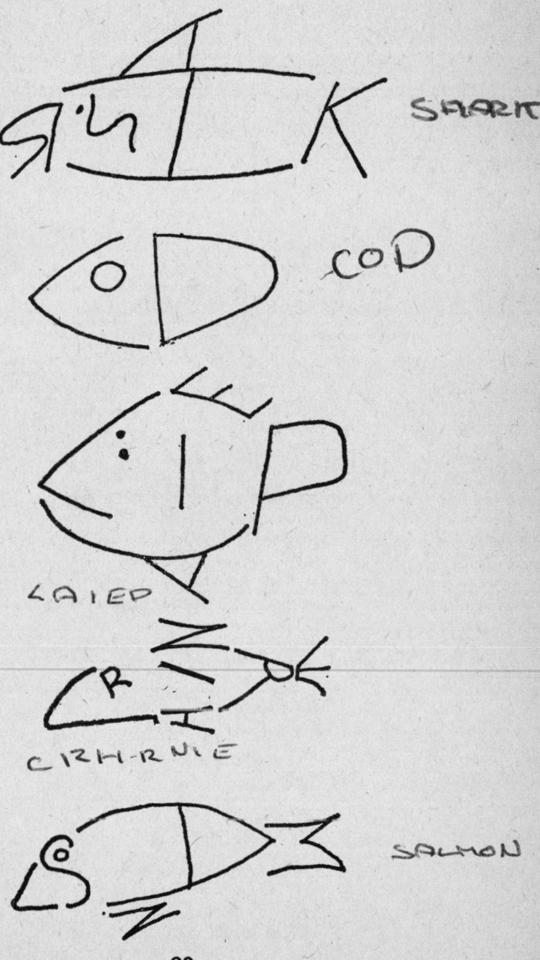

# The Hand
## by Spike Milligan

There was once a great classical piano player, Plink-Plank-Plonk. His name was Claudio Vilething. He made his world début at the Albert Hall playing Grieg's A minor piano concerto by Eileen Joyce, Plink-Plank-Plonk. Alas, came World War I, Boom-Bang-Crash. During hand to hand fighting, Wallop-Blatt-Thud, he was wounded in the hand he played the piano with, Plink-Plank-Silence. The Doctor was jealous of Claudio's genius and said the hand would have to be amputated, Chip-Chop-Chap. After the War the Doctor gloated over the hand, Gloat-Gloat-Gloat. One night the hand lost its temper, it strangled the Doctor. And the hand lived happily ever after, Laugh-Laugh-Laugh.

*Story written by hand.*

### Thing No. 5

Here, have you ever tried this?

Pull your lower eyelids downwards with your fore-finger and third finger of your left hand, and at the same time push the end of your nose upwards with the middle finger.

This leaves your right hand free to do something equally daft with your mouth or your cheeks or some-thing.

It looks revolting.

**Thing No. 6**

## BODY-BUILDING

For this you will need:—

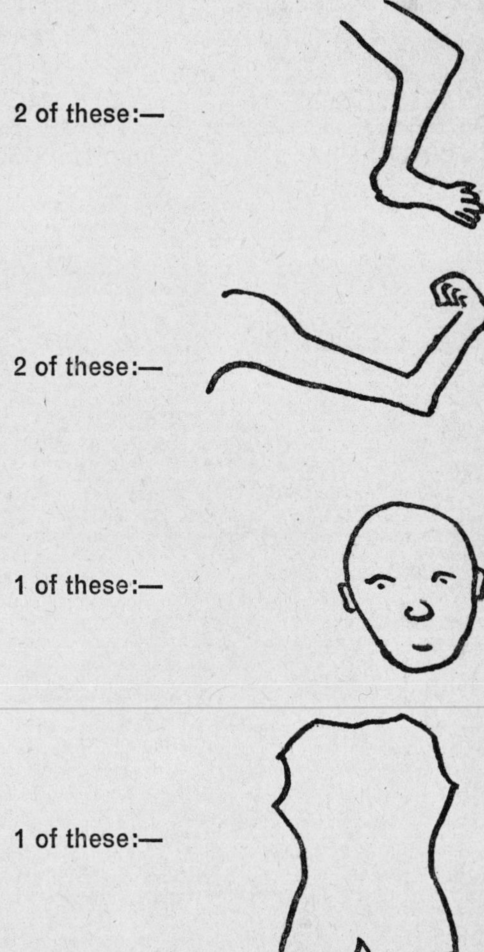

# The Puzzled Cat

Guess the following words. They all begin with *cat*.

A cat that is livestock.

A cat that is a firework.

A cat that is a larva.

A cat that is a disruption.

A cat that is to capture.

A cat that is religious instruction by question and answer.

A cat that is a cold.

A cat that is a subterranean cemetery.

A cat that is a disastrous end.

A cat that is the principal church of the diocese.

A cat that is a class.

A cat that is a complete list.

A cat that is a forked stick and elastic.

A cat that is the string of a violin.

A cat that provides food.

A cat that is a waterfall.

A cat that is infectious.

A cat that is a flower of some trees.

A cat that is a plant.

A cat that is a girl's name.

## Finding a Number Thought Of

Let somebody think of a number but tell him not to name it. Tell him to multiply it by three and add one to the result. Now let the sum be multiplied by three again and to that add the number thought of. Let the result be declared. Then to know the figure thought of you merely take away the last number and the other or others will be the number thought of. Thus:

| | |
|---|---|
| Number thought of | 7 |
| Multiplied by 3 | 21 |
| Add one | 22 |
| Multiply by 3 | 66 |
| Add the number first thought of | 7 |
| Answer | (7)3 |

## Number Trick

Cut 16 little slips of paper; number them from 1–16 and arrange them in order on the table. Now ask a friend to think of any number up to 16.

Tell him you are going to tap the numbers, and ask him to count the first tap as one more than the number he thought of, adding on 1 for each tap until he has reached the number 25 when he is to stop you.

Suppose the number he thought of was 10, then he will call your first tap eleven, the second tap 12 and so on up to 25. Then he stops you and you can tell him the number he thought of, by counting the number of taps backwards from 25.

When you are tapping do not point to the numbers in order as you count back; it looks much more impressive to dodge about. When you are stopped you can at once point to the correct number.

## Soppy Signs

Outside a hairdressing shop:

WE CURL UP AND DYE FOR YOU.

Outside a shop selling tropical fish:

WET PETS.

Outside a house:

ANYONE IS WELCOME TO BORROW OUR LAWN MOWER, AS LONG AS HE DOESN'T TAKE IT OUT OF THE YARD.

At an intersection in the road:

CROSS ROAD
(BETTER HUMOUR IT).

Street sign:

TO AVOID THAT RUN DOWN FEELING, LOOK BOTH WAYS BEFORE CROSSING.

Sign in a golf club:

BACK SOON. GONE TO TEE.

Outside a dry cleaning shop:

WHEN YOUR CLOTHES AREN'T BECOMING TO YOU, YOU SHOULD BE COMING TO US.

# Strange Historical Facts

In the year 1639 on board an East-Indiaman sailing vessel, there were an English and a Dutch sailor, who tried to rival each other by their activity in ascending and descending the rigging. At last the English sailor astonished his competitor by standing with his heels in the air upon the truck-head of the main topgallant mast. The Dutchman endeavoured to do the same, but in the attempt fell to the deck from which with great difficulty he raised himself a little, and exclaimed 'There, my friend, can you do that!' whereupon he immediately expired.

In the reign of Charles I, a Mayor of Norwich actually sent a man to prison for saying that the Prince of Wales was born without a shirt!

George IV, whilst Regent, on one occasion forgot he was a gentleman. This was when he flung a glass of wine in Colonel Hamlyn's face saying 'Hamlyn, you are a blackguard!' The insulted officer could not return the compliment without committing something like treason. It was out of the question to challenge the Prince, whilst to let the insult pass unnoticed was equally impossible. The colonel filled his glass and threw the contents in the face of his neighbour, observing 'His Royal Highness's toast. Pass it on!'

---

George III was extremely punctual and expected punctuality from everyone about him. Lord Harris was the most punctual person who attended on His Majesty —he was never a second behind his time. One day he had an appointment with the King at twelve o'clock. On passing through the hall the clock struck twelve, at which his lordship, in a rage through being a minute or two late, raised his cane, and broke the glass of the clock. The King reminded him that he was a little beyond his time, which Lord Harris excused as well as he could.

At the next audience, the King, as he entered the room, exclaimed, 'Why, Harris, how came you to strike the clock?'

To which Harris replied, 'The clock struck first, your Majesty!'

# Historical Hysterics

*'Yes, I could do a party of ten for sixty pence per head.*

*'I wouldn't let MY kid go around with a haircut like that!'*

# Aunts and Uncles
## by Mervyn Peake

When Aunty Jane
Became a Crane
She put one leg behind her head;
And even when the clock struck ten
Refused to go to bed.

When Aunty Grace
Became a Plaice
She all but vanished sideways on;
Except her nose
And pointed toes
The rest of her was gone.

When Uncle Wog
Became a Dog
He hid himself for shame;
He sometimes hid his bone as well
And wouldn't hear the front-door bell,
Or answer to his name.

When Aunty Flo
Became a Crow
She had a bed put in the tree;
And there she lay
And read all day
Of ornithology.

When Aunty Vi
Became a Fly
Her favourite nephew
Sought her life;
How could he know
That with each blow
He bruised his Uncle's wife?

# Aunts and Uncles

When Uncle Sam
Became a Ham
We did not care to carve him up;
He struggled so;
We let him go
And gave him to the pup.

When Aunty Nag
Became a Crag
She stared across the dawn,
To where her spouse
Kept open house
With ladies on the lawn.

When Aunty Mig
Became a Pig
She floated on the briny breeze,
With irritation in her heart
And warts upon her knees.

When Aunty Jill
Became a Pill
She stared all day through dark-blue glass;
And always sneered
When men appeared
To ask her how she was.

When Uncle Jake
Became a Snake
He never found it out;
And so as no one mentions it
One sees him still about.

# Hey, Waiter!

**Waiter:** 'How did you find your steak, sir?'

**Diner:** 'Just by accident. I moved the baked potato and there it was.'

**Tom:** 'How do you make soup gold?'

**Tim:** 'You put in fourteen carrots.'

'Is she Hungary?' Henry asked.

'Alaska,' said Harry.

'Yes, Siam,' she replied.

'All right, I'll Fiji,' Henry offered.

'Oh don't Russia,' Harry admonished.

'What if she Wales?' Henry demanded.

'Give her some Chile,' Harry suggested.

'I'd rather have Turkey,' she said, 'except that I can't have any Greece.'

When the waiter brought the check, Harry asked Henry, 'How much has Egypt you?'

'Tough luck,' said the egg in the monastery. 'Out of the frying-pan into the Friar.'

Why is a hot dog the noblest of dogs?
*Because it feeds the hand that bites it.*

# Find the Colour

What colours should go in the spaces?

The _ _ _ _ _ Cliffs of Dover

_ _ _ Admiral Butterfly

The _ _ _ _ _ Hole of Calcutta

The _ _ _ _ _ _ _ Pimpernel

Little Boy _ _ _ _

_ _ _ _ _ with envy

A _ _ _ _ _ _ streak of cowardice

In a _ _ _ _ _ study

Lady Jane _ _ _ _

# Find the Creature

Find the creatures by removing one letter from the following words. For example, *hoarse* becomes *horse* by removing the letter *a.*

clock
peony
bowl
beard
cart
ping
gloat
then
steal
bath

# Travel Sick

'That new route with the low bridge was a piece of cake.'

'Well, you asked us to pass Father down the bus!'

'No, mine's not among that lot—I'll try St. Pancras!'

# Two-faced Puzzle

FIND THE HARE

FIND THE MERRY MAN

FIND THE MAN'S DAUGHTER

FIND THE CLOWN

FIND THE FAT BOY

FIND THE FOX

FIND THE BOY'S FATHER

FIND THE SOLDIER

FIND THE SWAN

# Epilaughs

Here are some weird epitaphs taken from gravestones:

Here lie I, bereft of breath,
Because a cough
Carried me off;
Then a coffin
They carried me off in.

Here lie the bones of Richard Lawton,
Whose death, alas! was strangely brought on.
Trying one day his corns to mow off,
The razor slipped and cut his toe off;
His toe, or rather what it grew to,
An inflammation quickly flew to,
Which took alas to mortifying,
And was the cause of Richard's dying.

*From Old Greyfriars, Edinburgh.*

## Epilaughs

Here snug in grave my wife doth lie;
Now she's at rest and so am I!

Here lies an honest lawyer,
And that's *Strange*.

*Epitaph on a lawyer named Mr. Strange*

### On a Smoker

Here, fast asleep, full six feet deep,
And seventy summers ripe,
George Thompson lies, in hopes to rise
And smoke another pipe.

This man by worms was fed,
The worms procured him fish,
But now that he is dead,
The worms will have the dish.

### On a Vicar of Kendal

London bred me, Westminster fed me,
Cambridge sped me, my cousin wed me,
Study taught me, Kendal caught me,
Labour pressed me, sickness distressed
Death oppressed me, the grave possessed.
God first made me, Christ did save me,
Earth did crave me, but Heaven has me.

## And those elephant jokes . . .

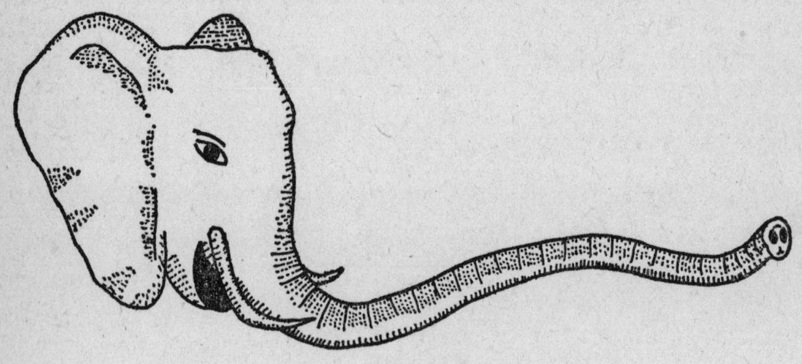

How does an elephant get down from a tree?
*He climbs on a leaf and waits for autumn.*

What did the grape say when the elephant stepped on it?
*Nothing, it just let out a little whine.*

How can you tell if an elephant has been in your refrigerator?
*You can see his footprints in the butter.*

What time it is when an elephant sits on a fence?
*Time to buy a new one.*

What is the difference between a flea and an elephant?
*An elephant can have fleas, but a flea can't have elephants.*

Why do elephants wear dark glasses?
*If you had all those jokes told about you, you wouldn't want to be recognised either!*

What is the difference between an elephant and a bison?
*You can't wash your hands in an elephant!*

What would you get if you crossed an elephant with a mouse?

*Huge holes in your skirting boards!*

Two elephants fell off a cliff.

*Boom! Boom!*

How would an elephant smell without his trunk?

*He'd still smell!*

How can five elephants be got into your car?

*Two in the front and three in the back!*

Why did the eleph and the ant get married?

*They wanted to have eleph-ants!*

Why does an elephant have a trunk?

*So that he can hide himself away in it when he spots a mouse.*

Why are elephants flat-footed?

*They're always jumping up and down with enthusiasm!*

# Observation Test

Here are twelve objects. Study them for one minute, then list those you can remember. (No peeping.)

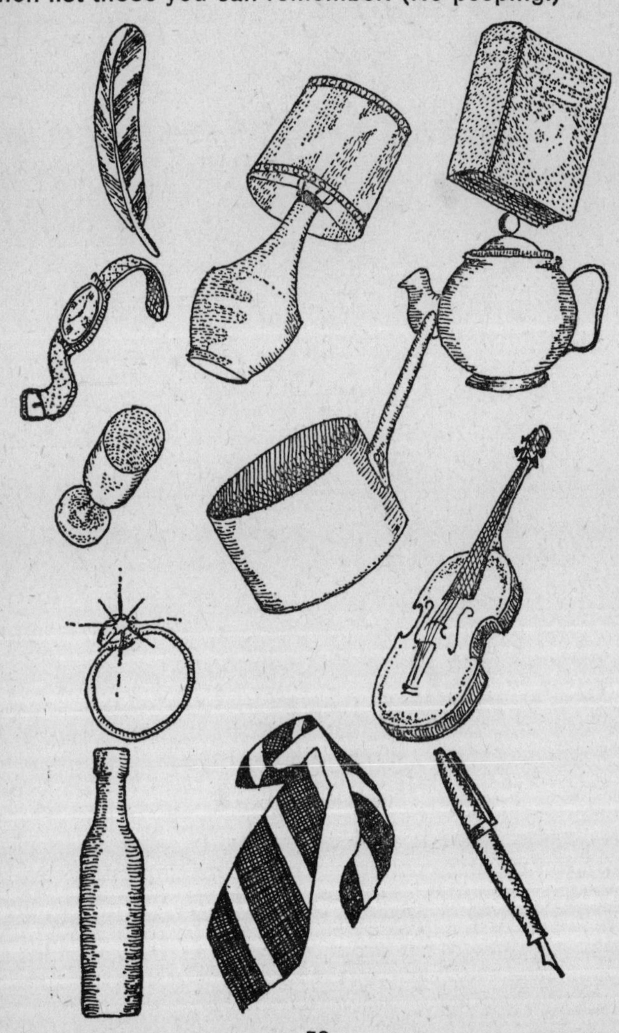

# The King's Breakfast
## by A. A. Milne

The King asked
The Queen, and
The Queen asked
The Dairymaid:
'Could we have some butter for
The Royal slice of bread?'
The Queen asked
The Dairymaid,
The Dairymaid
Said, 'Certainly,
I'll go and tell
The cow
Now
Before she goes to bed.'

The Dairymaid
She curtsied,
And went and told
The Alderney:
'Don't forget the butter for
The Royal slice of bread.'

The Alderney
Said sleepily:
'You'd better tell
His Majesty
That many people nowadays
Like marmalade
Instead.'

The Dairymaid
Said, 'Fancy!'
And went to Her Majesty.
She curtsied to the Queen, and
She turned a little red:
'Excuse me,
Your Majesty,
For taking of
The liberty,
But marmalade is tasty, if
It's very
Thickly spread.'

The Queen said,
'Oh!'
And went to
His Majesty:
'Talking of the butter for
The Royal slice of bread,
Many people
Think that
Marmalade
Is nicer.
Would you like to try a little
Marmalade
Instead?'

The King said,
'Bother!'
And then he said,
'Oh, deary me!'
The King sobbed, 'Oh, deary me!'
And went back to bed.

'Nobody,'
He whimpered,
'Could call me
A fussy man;
I *only* want
A little bit
Of butter for
My bread!'

The Queen said,
'There, there!'
And went to
The Dairymaid.
The Dairymaid
Said, 'There, there!'
And went to the shed.
The cow said,
'There, there!
I didn't really
Mean it;
Here's milk for his porringer
And butter for his bread.'

The Queen took
The butter
And brought it to
His Majesty;
The King said,
'Butter, eh?'
And bounced out of bed.
'Nobody,' he said,
As he kissed her
Tenderly,

'Nobody,' he said,
As he slid down
The banister,
'Nobody,
My darling,
Could call me
A fussy man—
BUT
*'I do like a little bit of butter to my bread!'*

# Ninepence Puzzle

Here is a puzzle that is not at all difficult to solve. All you need is nine pennies—or if you haven't got nine pennies, counters, beans or small stones will do.

Arrange the nine pence in rows as shown here.

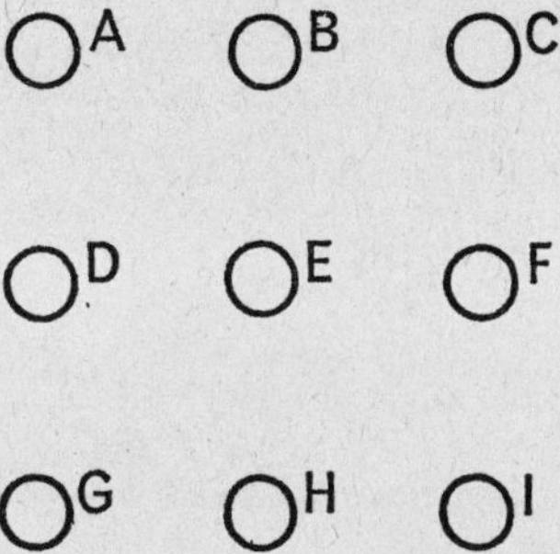


Look carefully at this simple arrangement of the coins, and see how many rows each containing 3 coins there are.

The puzzle is to move only 2 of the pennies so as to make 10 rows each consisting of 3 coins. It is useful to notice when tackling this puzzle that in the arrangement of the coins shown here, the coins running diagonally AEI and CEG form 2 rows of 3 in a row.

**Thing No. 7**

## A FUNNY JOKE

Slice yourself down the middle with a home-made circular saw.

Then walk into a room and say:

(All right then—'*hop* into a room . . .')

**Thing No. 8**

## ANOTHER MERRY WHEEZE

When the rest of the family is out in the kitchen, close the door carefully so they can't see what you are up to.

Then take all your clothes off, put the coal-scuttle on your head and climb on top of the television set.

Then call out, 'Quick everyone—there's something very unusual on the telly tonight!'

# Pair the Words

Pair up the words on the left with those on the right: e.g., Cup Board—Cupboard.

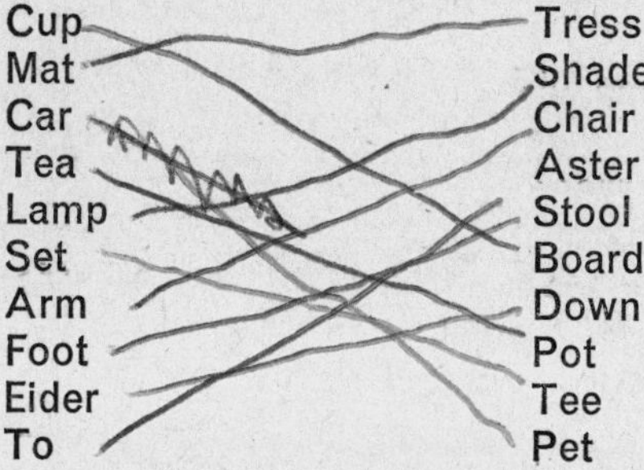

| | |
|---|---|
| Cup | Tress |
| Mat | Shade |
| Car | Chair |
| Tea | Aster |
| Lamp | Stool |
| Set | Board |
| Arm | Down |
| Foot | Pot |
| Eider | Tee |
| To | Pet |

Can you find the link between these pairs of words? You will find that one word will replace both: e.g., Acrobat/Glass—Tumbler.

| | | |
|---|---|---|
| Acrobat | Tumbler | Glass |
| Bobbin | Reel | Dance |
| Beak | | Account |
| Sphere | Round | Dance |
| Reign | | Measure |
| Book | | Amount |
| Orchestra | | Ribbon |
| Ghost | | Alcohol |
| Pip | | Weight |

# Daft Definitions

| | |
|---|---|
| *Astronomer* | A night watchman. |
| *Depth* | Height turned upside down. |
| *Archaeologist* | A man whose career lies in ruins. |
| *Bacteria* | The rear entrance to a cafeteria. |
| *Skeleton* | Someone inside out with his outside off. |
| *Psychiatrist* | A man who doesn't have to worry as long as other people do. |
| *A caterpillar* | An upholstered worm. |
| *Undercover agent* | A spy in bed. |
| *Etiquette* | Saying 'No, thank you' when you want to say yes. |
| *Sick reptile* | Illigator. |
| *Icicle* | Eavesdropper. |
| *Mosquito* | A flying hypodermic needle. |
| *Conference* | A meeting of the bored. |
| *Suit of armour* | Knightgown. |
| *Rubber gloves* | Things you can put on and then wash your hands without getting them wet. |
| *Cannibal* | A person who is fed up with people. |

# An Amazing Puzzle

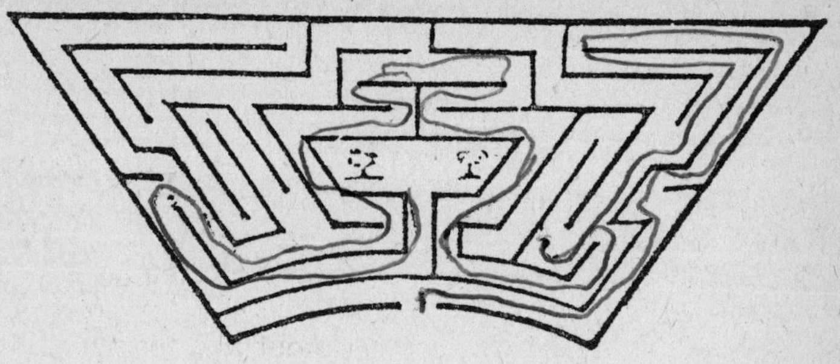

A MAZE OR LABYRINTH. — This maze is a correct ground-plan of one in the gardens of the Palace of Hampton Court. No legendary tale is attached to it, of which we are aware, but its labyrinthine walks occasion much amusement to the numerous holiday-makers who frequent the palace grounds. The partitions between the walks are hedges of clipped hornbeam, and are about five feet in height. The puzzle is to get into the centre, where seats are placed under two lofty trees, and many are the disappointments experienced before the end is attained; and even then the trouble is not over, it being quite as difficult to get out as to get in.

Can you find your way in—and out?

# History Howlers

Mary Queen of Scots had previously been married to the Dolphin. (Dauphin)

Queen Philippa saved the lives of six honest burglars of Calais. (Burghers)

Because he would not obey the King, Cranmer was threatened with the steak. (stake)

Charles I married the Infant of Spain. (Infanta)

The peasants revolted against the King because he oppressed them with heavy taxis. (taxes)

Julius Caesar was told to beware the Brides of March. (Ides)

Fluorescence Nightingale was known as the lady of the lamp. (Florence)

1066 was the year of the Mormon invasion. (Norman)

What did George Washington's father say when George brought home his school report?

*Why did you go down in history?*

## More Riddles

With what two animals do you always go to bed?
*Two calves.*

How many hairs in a rabbit's tail?
*None. They are all outside.*

When the clock strikes 13, what time is it?
*Time to get it fixed.*

What is bought by the yard and worn by the foot?
*Carpet.*

Why is your nose not 12 inches long?
*Because it would then be a foot.*

How many balls of string would it take to reach the moon?
*One, if it were long enough.*

What is yours, and used by others more than yourself?
*Your name.*

Which is the oldest tree?
*The elder.*

What do liars do after death?
*Lie still.*

What goes uphill and downhill, and always stays in the same place?
*A road.*

What falls often, but never gets hurt?
*Snow.*

# Don't be a Clown

*'I don't know what's come over him—he never used to have a temper like this!'*

*'It's a good act, but I have to keep buying new dogs!'*

## Back to the Classroom

*'So that leaves YOU top of the class.'*

During a history lesson a teacher asked, 'What do you know of Margaret of Anjou?'

'She was very fat, sir,' answered one boy.

This was new to the teacher, and he asked the lad from where he had got that information.

'It's in this book I've got here, sir,' he said. 'Amongst Henry's stoutest supporters was Margaret of Anjou.'

**Teacher:** 'How is it you were not at school yesterday, Johnny?'

**Johnny:** 'Please, sir, when I was coming down the street I saw a steam-roller.'

**Teacher:** 'Well what about it?'

**Johnny:** 'A man touched me on the shoulder and said, "Mind that steam roller". And I stood minding it all day!'

**Teacher:** 'Now, Tommy, what's an anecdote?'

**Tommy:** 'A short, funny tail, sir.'

**Teacher:** 'Correct. Now give me a sentence containing the word.'

**Tommy:** 'A rabbit is an animal with four legs and one anecdote.'

# Limericks by Edward Lear

There was an old person of Dean
Who dined on one pea and one bean;
For he said, 'More than that, would make me too fat,'
That cautious old person of Dean.

There was an old man in a tree,
Whose whiskers were lovely to see;
But the birds of the air, pluck'd them perfectly bare,
To make themselves nests in that tree.

# Find the Twins

Only two of the pictures beneath are identical. Can you discover them?

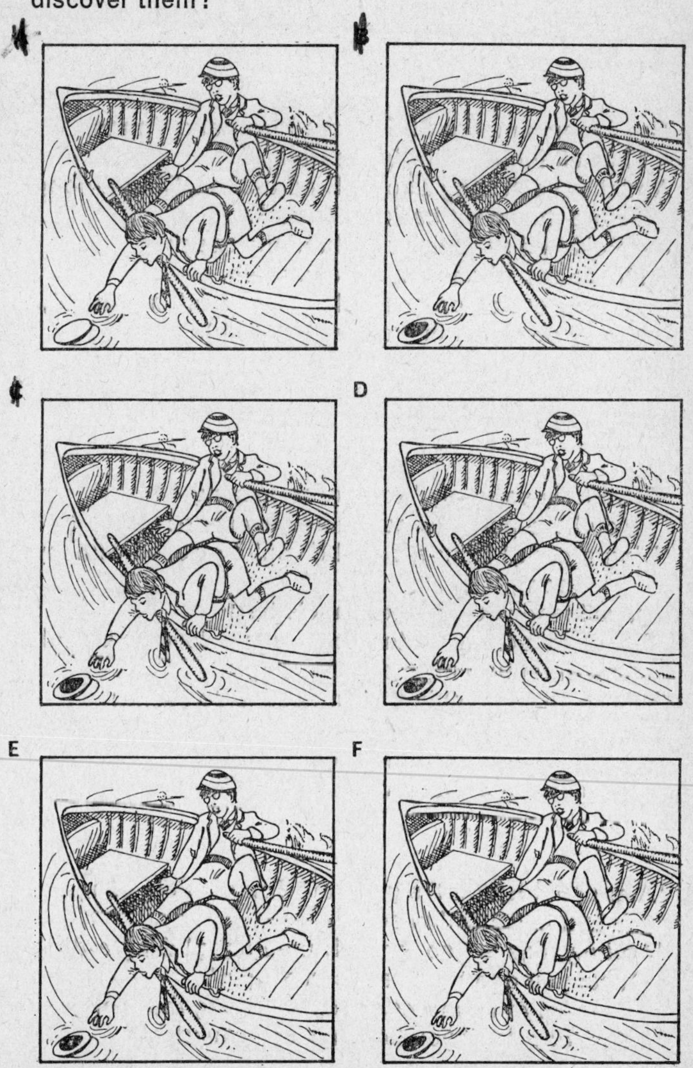

# The Broom, the Shovel, the Poker and the Tongs

## by Edward Lear

I

The Broom and the Shovel, the Poker and Tongs,
They all took a drive in the Park,
And they each sang a song, Ding-a-dong, Ding-a-dong,
Before they went back in the dark.
Mr. Poker he sat quite upright in the coach,
Mr. Tongs made a clatter and clash,
Miss Shovel was dressed all in black (with a brooch),
Mrs. Broom was in blue (with a sash).
Ding-a-dong! Ding-a-dong!
And they all sang a song!

II

'O Shovely so lovely!' the Poker he sang,
'You have perfectly conquered my heart!
'Ding-a-dong! Ding-a-dong! If you're pleased with my
song,
'I will feed you with cold apple tart!
'When you scrape on the coals with a delicate sound,
'You enrapture my life with delight!
'Your nose is so shiny! Your head is so round!
'And your shape is so slender and bright!
'Ding-a-dong! Ding-a-dong!
'Ain't you pleased with my song?'

III

'Alas! Mrs. Broom!' sighed the Tongs in his song,
'O is it because I'm so thin,
'And my legs are so long—Ding-a-dong! Ding-a-dong!
'That you don't care about me a pin?
'Ah fairest of creatures, when sweeping the room,
'Ah! why don't you heed my complaint!

'Must you needs be so cruel, you beautiful Broom,
  'Because you are covered with paint?
    'Ding-a-dong! Ding-a-dong!

## IV

Mrs. Broom and Miss Shovel together they sang,
  'What nonsense you're singing to-day!'
Said the Shovel, 'I'll certainly hit you a bang!'
  Said the Broom, 'And I'll sweep you away!'
So the Coachman drove homeward as fast as he could,
  Perceiving their anger with pain;
But they put on the kettle, and little by little,
  They all became happy again.
    Ding-a-dong!
    There's an end of my song!

# Tonguetwisters

A pale pink proud peacock pompously preened its pretty plumage.

A pleasant place to place plaice is a place where the plaice are pleased to be placed.

The brisk brave brigadiers brandished broad bright blades, blunderbusses and bludgeons.

Can you imagine an imaginary menagerie manager imagining managing an imaginary menagerie?

Mister Matthew Mathers, my maths master, munches mashed marmalade muffins.

Which is the witch that wished the wicked wish?

A cricket critic cricked his neck at a critical cricket match.

If a chicken and a half  
Laid an egg and a half  
In a day and a half,  
The farmer wouldn't half have a fit and a half.

# Word Squares

Try to find the words in the following letter puzzles. For example:

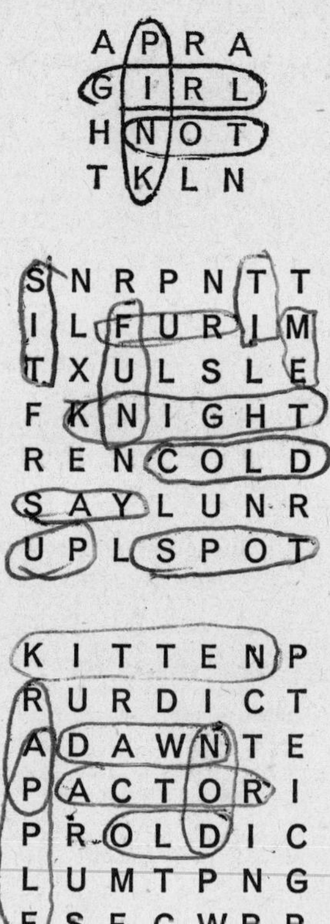

### Thing No. 9

## HOW TO MAKE JUMPING BEANS

Get some beans, go up behind them very quietly and say 'Boo!'

### Thing No. 10

## HOW TO GET BLOOD OUT OF A STONE

If it hasn't been in there very long you can pour it out. Otherwise you will just have to poke around with a pin or a hair-grip or something and scrape it out in bits.

Beats me how it got in there in the first place.

# Meet your Match

A man had to light a bonfire, a gas stove, and a geyser in the bathroom, and also light his cigarette, and he only had one match. Which did he light first?

*The match of course!*

Can you make $2\frac{1}{2}$ dozen matches out of 8 matches?

Most people try to do it by making Roman numerals. Well this is how you do it.

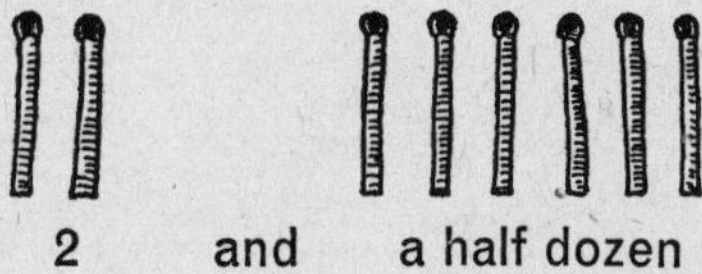


Try this one out on those of your friends who think they are strong. Put a match on the top of your head and place your hand over it. Then ask any of your friends if he can lift your hand off the match (lift, not push). It is almost impossible even for a very strong man.

## . . . and yet more giggles

Did you ever hear about the man who kept on banging his head against a brick wall?

*Well, you see, he found it was so nice when he stopped!*

Gestapo officer to prisoners-of-war . . .
'Today we will have a cross-country run. The first back and the last back will be shot. Right, off you go, you two.'

Why do little birds in a nest always agree?

*Because if they did not they would fall out!*

POLICE NOTICE
Man wanted for burglary—apply within.

What would be the best thing to do if you were mad?

*Change your mind.*

Private Jones, who wore thirteens in boots, was missing when the roll was called.

'Has anyone seen Jones?' bellowed the sergeant.

'Yes,' said a voice. 'He's gone up to the crossroads to turn round.'

Two men at a signpost: 'How long does it say?'

'Ten miles.'

'Well, then. Doing it together that'll be five miles each between us.'

What did one candle say to the other?

*You're getting on my wick.*

**Angry Businessman:** 'Get out! I can't see you today!'

**Salesman:** 'That's excellent, sir. I'm selling spectacles.'

# Seaside Picture Puzzle

Discover what can be seen at the seaside by taking the first letter of each object that you see in the squares and building up a word using letters already supplied.

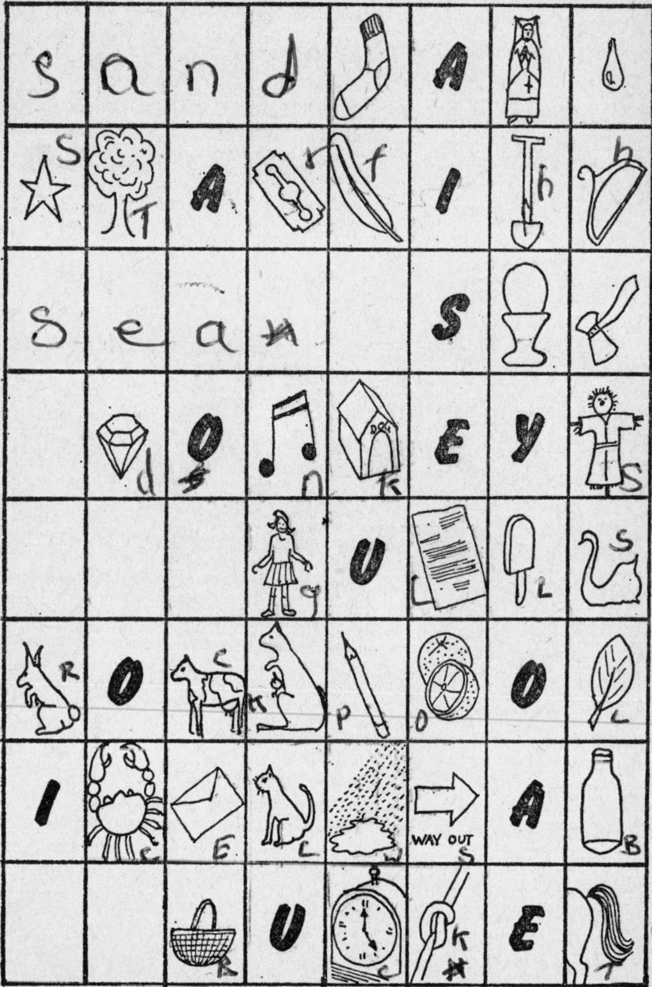

# More Animal Antics

Hide, you idiot, we're supposed to be extinct!'

Are you going to get in or do I have to throw you in?'

**Thing No. 11**

## DO-IT-YOURSELF MEDICINE

(i)

This man:

a. has the 'flu.
b. has a broken leg.
c. is drunk.

(ii)

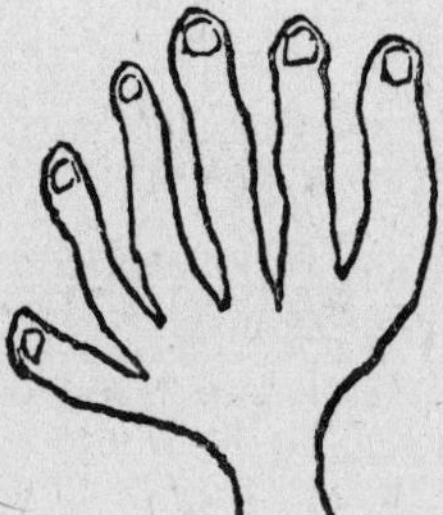

What would you suggest in a case like this:

a. amputation.
b. decimalisation.
c. a recount.

(iii)

This lady is suffering from:

a. cramp.
b. delusions.
c. deafness.
d. loose ears.

*'. . . and stop calling me Dad!'*

*'Please can Gilbert come out to pray?'*

## Wine and Water Trick

In a wine glass half full of water, drop a piece of bread as big as the top of your finger. Gently pour some wine upon it, and miraculously the two liquids will remain separate, the water remaining at the bottom of the glass and the wine floating on its surface.

## To Turn a Glass of Water Upside Down

This is an extremely good trick when performed well. Fill a glass with water, lay a piece of paper on the top of it, and place the palm of your hand flat on the paper and press closely down. Then take hold of the foot of the glass with the right hand, and invert the position of the glass, still pressing the paper close with the left hand. Hold it in this manner for a minute or two and then withdraw the left hand, when the paper will be found to have stuck to the glass.

Explanation: The pressure of air underneath, acting against the paper with a superior weight to that of the water, is sufficient to retain it in its position, and consequently sustain the water in the glass.

# Questions, Quistions and Quostions
## by Spike Milligan

Daddy how does an elephant feel
When he swallows a piece of steel?
Does he get drunk
And fall on his trunk
Or roll down the road like a wheel?

Daddy what would a pelican do
If he swallowed a bottle of glue?
Would his beak get stuck
Would he run out of luck
And lose his job at the zoo?

Son tell me tell me true.
If I belted you with a shoe,
Would you fall down dead?
Would you go up to bed?
—Either of those would do.

# Sneaky Bill
## by William Cole

I'm Sneaky Bill, I'm terrible mean and vicious,
I steal all the cashews from the mixed-nuts dishes;
I eat all the icing but I won't touch the cake,
And what you won't give me, I'll go ahead and take.
I gobble up the cherries from everyone's drinks,
And if there's sausages I grab a dozen links;
I take both drumsticks if there's turkey or chicken,
And the biggest strawberries are what I'm pickin'.
I make sure I get the finest chop on the plate
And I'll eat the portions of anyone who's late!

I'm always on the spot before the dinner bell—
I guess I'm pretty awful,
but
I
do
eat
well!

## Hunt the Animal

Try to find the animals from these jumbled words.

XOF
ATB
NIMREE
VRABEE
RUGAJA
SAS
PAOLEDR
RAFIFEG
NILO
KACLJA
REAH
TOPPOPHUSAIM
MALAL
TARMOM

NUGEIPAGI
RULWAS
GEOGDEHH
HELAW
RESHO
XYON
TELPNEHA
REBA
SEPHE
MGNEILM
GESNMOOO
HATRENP
PURPONECI
NOBABO

## and try this one . . .

Re-arrange these words to make objects found in the classroom.

bradocklab
clenip
lerru
stpurec
sked
obok
khalc

## And More Limericks

There was an old man in a trunk,
Who inquired of his wife: 'Am I drunk?'
  She replied with regret:
  'I'm afraid so, my pet.'
And he answered: 'It's just as I thunk.'

*Ogden Nash*

A wonderful bird is the pelican;
His bill can hold more than his belican.
  He can take in his beak
  Food enough for a week;
But I'm damned if I see how the helican!

*Dixon Lanier Merritt*

There was a young lady of Ryde
Who ate a green apple and died;
  The apple fermented
  Inside the lamented,
And made cider inside her inside. *Anon.*

There was an old person of Lyme
Who married three wives at a time.
  When asked: 'Why the third?'
  He replied: 'One's absurd,
And bigamy, sir, is a crime.' *Anon.*

There was a faith-healer of Deal,
Who said: 'Although pain isn't real,
  If I sit on a pin
  And it punctures my skin,
I dislike what I fancy I feel.' *Anon.*

There was a young man of Devizes
Whose ears were of different sizes;
  The one that was small
  Was no use at all,
But the other won several prizes. *Anon.*

# Knitting-needle Puzzle

Here are seven balls of wool. The problem is to lay three knitting-needles so that they separate all the balls from each other. Try it with buttons instead of wool, if you prefer.

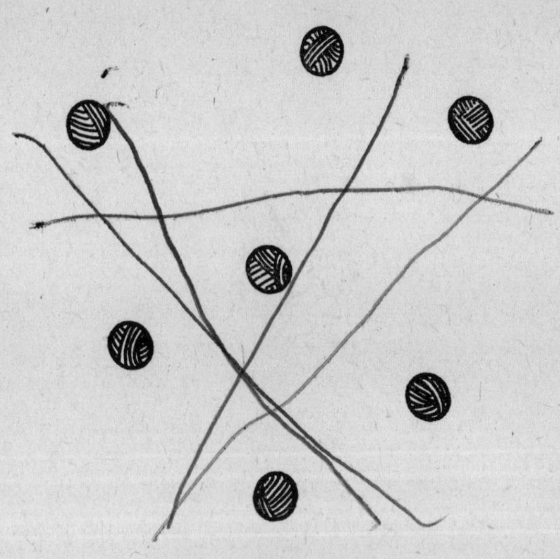

# Hysterical Historics

'Say XCIX.'

'Haven't you finished ironing my trousers yet?'

# It's a Laugh . . .

Never buy a cheap violin—it might be a fiddle.

POLICE NOTICE

Will the motorist who took the fourth turning of the M2, please put it back!

Do you know what you look like when you are asleep?
*Well, if not, look in the mirror with your eyes shut.*

## Serve Him Right

'Prisoner,' said the judge. 'Have you anything to say before I pass sentence?'

'Assuredly, my lord,' replied the highly-educated prisoner. 'I desire to state, without reserve or circumlocution, that the penalty imposed should be in keeping or as it were commensurate with my station in life which I assure you has hitherto been of no inconsiderable importance.'

'Well, you seem to have a liking for long sentences. Ten years,' was the judge's comment.

Where does a frog hang his coat?
*In a croakroom!*

An Irishman wished to commit suicide because of the dreadful misfortunes that had befallen him. But to save his family from possible disgrace, he left the following note on his table.

> 'I hope you will not think that I committed suicide. My death is the result of an accident. The pistol went off as I was cleaning it.'

**Taxi-driver** (to policeman): 'Somebody's left this kipper in my cab, officer. What shall I do with it?'

**Policeman:** 'Leave it here, and if it is not claimed in 6 months, it's yours.'

## Riddle-me-ree

What is the longest yet the shortest thing in the world, the swiftest yet the slowest, the most divisible and the most extended, the least valued and the most regretted, without which nothing can be done—which devours everything, however small, and yet gives life and spirits to every object, however great?

*Time.*

Why are feet like old tales?

*Because they are leg-ends.*

Why is a tight boot like an oak tree?

*Because it produces a-corn.*

What is the last thing you take off, before you go to bed?

*Your feet from the floor.*

Why do footballers keep so cool?

*They have a lot of fans.*

Why can the world never come to an end?

*Because it is round.*

What do you find inside a Chinese mouse's mouth?

*A Mao se Tung.*

Where does a ghost train stop?

*At a manifestation.*

# Rabbit Maze

Which rabbit found his way home?

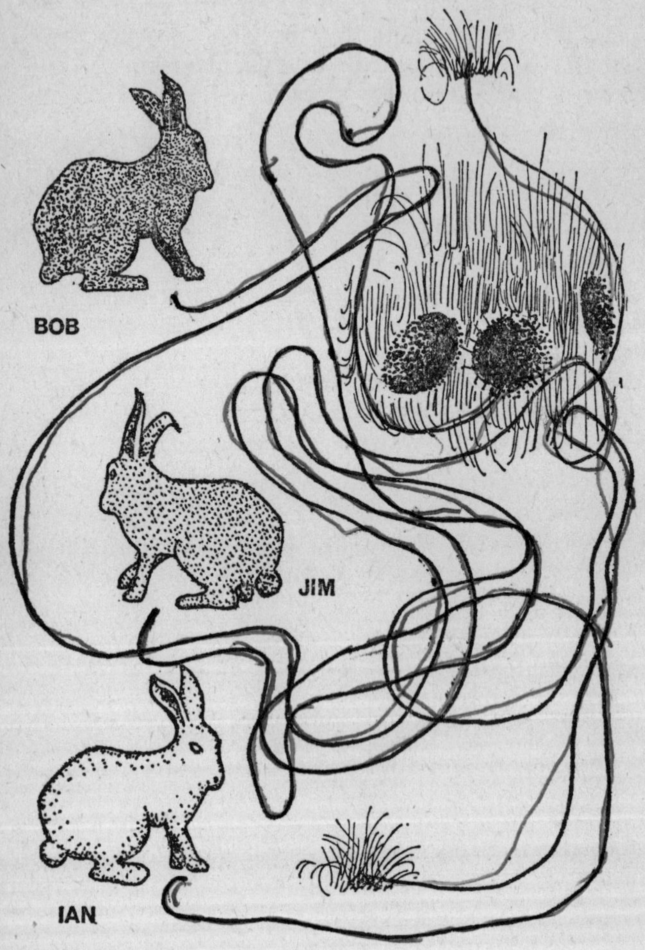

**Thing No. 12**

## HOW TO DO LION-TAMING

You will need some, or all, of the following:

(i) a bent-wood chair, light enough to hold out in front of you with one hand.
(ii) a whip.
(iii) an hypnotic stare or a loaded hypodermic syringe.
(iv) a long splinter of wood and a pair of tweezers.
(v) a lion.

Method A:

Face the lion and fix him with your hypnotic stare, or your hypodermic, saying 'You are tame, you are tame, you are tame.'

Method B:

Face the lion, holding the bent-wood chair straight out in front of you, and say 'If you don't do as I tell you I'm going to stick the leg of this chair right up your nose.'

Method C:

When he's not looking, place the splinter of wood on the floor of the lion's cage. Sooner or later he'll get this stuck in his paw. Then, when you step fearlessly forward with your tweezers and remove the splinter he'll probably be ever so grateful. If not, you can always use Method B, holding the chair with your *good* arm.

**Thing No. 13**

## HOW TO ENJOY YOUR MEASLES

Measles is like lightning. (Or should that be 'measles *are* like lightning'?)

Measles never strikes in the same spot twice. What it does do, of course, is to strike once in lots of spots.

It's not very nice, so don't go out of your way to get it just for the sake of doing this 'Thing'; still, if you do catch it you might as well get what fun you can out of it. Here are two suggestions:

(i) Get your friends to guess how many spots you have. They could all pay a penny a guess, then the one nearest to the right number would get all the money. The one nearest to *you* would probably get measles. By the time his spots were in full bloom, you would be back on your feet and able to join in the fun and games, guessing how many spots *he's* got.

(ii) Use a felt-tip pen to join the spots to form the picture of a well-known personality; or of somebody you really like; or (if you use a mirror) somebody you really *don't* like.

**Thing No. 14**

## MORE FIRST AID HINTS

How to deal with water on the knee

That's it—you just give it a little tap.

**Thing No. 15**

## HOW TO MAKE THE MOST OF YOURSELF

After blocking up all other apertures, stick an air-pump up your left nostril.

## The Three Spoons

This is an excellent trick but requires a friend's help. Place three silver spoons crosswise on the table and request any person to touch one and tell him that you will find out the one he has touched by a single look, even though you are outside the room when he does so. You leave the room and when he tells you to come back, you walk up to the table and inspect the spoons as if trying to ascertain whether there are any finger marks upon them, and then decide.

Your confederate, of course, makes some sign previously agreed on to give you the clue to the spoon. This may be done by touching a button on his coat for the top spoon, touching his chin for the second and putting his finger to his lips to signify the lowest. The precise actions are up to you to agree on.

## The Magic Apple

Pass a needle and thread under the rind of a soft apple, which is easily done by putting the needle in again at the same hole it came out of, and so passing it on until you have gone right round the apple. Then take both ends of the thread in your hands and carefully pull them so as to draw the middle portion of the thread through the apple which will then be divided in two parts. By repeating the process you may divide the fruit into as many parts as you please, without breaking the rind. The apple may be given to someone to peel, and as soon as the rind is removed it will fall to pieces!

## Sick Humour

**Doctor:** 'How do you feel today, after your accident? You know you broke some ribs.'

**Patient:** 'Yes. I'm all right, but I've got stitch in my side.'

**Doctor:** 'Don't worry—shows the bones are knitting.'

**Doctor:** 'If anything comes to worry you, just cast it aside.'

**Patient:** 'All right, doc, I'll remember your advice when your bill comes.'

**Child:** 'Mummy, mummy, I feel as sick as a dog.'

**Mother:** 'Oh dear! I'd better go and ring for the vet.'

## Black Currant Jam

Greedy boy—
  Pot of jam—
Cupboard—joy!
  Boy cram.

Very sick—
  Take a pill—
Doctor quick!
  Boy ill.

Enter nurse—
  Put to bed—
Bad—worse!
  Boy dead!

## Old Mrs Thing-um-e-bob
## by Charles Causley

Old Mrs Thing-um-e-bob,
  Lives at you-know-where,
Dropped her what-you-may-call-it down
  The well of the kitchen stair.

'Gracious me!' said Thing-um-e-bob,
  'This don't look too bright.
I'll ask old Mr What's-his-name
  To try and put it right.'

Along came Mr What's-his-name,
  He said, 'You've broke the lot!
I'll have to see what I can do
  With some of the you-know-what.'

So he gave the what-you-may-call-it a pit
  And he gave it a bit of a pat,
And he put it all together again
  With a little of this and that.

And he gave the what-you-may-call-it a dib
  And he gave it a dab as well
When all of a sudden he heard a note
  As clear as any bell.

'It's as good as new!' cried What's-his-name.
  'But please remember, now,
In future Mrs Thing-um-e-bob
  You'll have to go you-know-how.'

## King Foo Foo
## by Charles Causley

King Foo Foo sat upon his throne
Dressed in his royal closes,
While all around his courtiers stood
With clothes-pegs on their noses.

'This action strange,' King Foo Foo said,
'My mind quite discomposes,
Though vulgar curiosity
A good king never shoses.'

But to the court it was as clear
As poetry or prose is:
King Foo Foo had not had a bath
Since goodness only knoses.

But one fine day the Fire Brigade
Rehearsing with their hoses
(To Handel's 'Water Music' played
With many puffs and bloses)

Quite failed the water to control
In all its ebbs and floses
And simply drenched the King with sev-
Eral thousand gallon doses.

At this each wight (though impolite)
A mighty grin exposes.
'At last,' the King said, 'now I see
That all my court morose is!'

'A debt to keep his courtiers gay
A monarch surely owses,
And deep within my royal breast
A sporting heart reposes.'

So now each night its water bright
The Fire Brigade disposes
Over a King who smiles as sweet
As all the royal roses.

# Back to the Circus

'He always takes hiccups terribly badly.'

# Food for Laughter

**Diner:** 'Hey, waiter! I can't eat this turkey. Call the manager!'

**Waiter:** 'It's no use, sir. He won't eat it either.'

**Customer:** 'Is there any soup on the menu?'

**New Waiter:** 'Not now, sir. I wiped it off.'

**Young child in restaurant in France:** 'Mummy, please may I have some frogs' legs?'

**Mother:** 'Why? What's the matter with your own?'

**Lady:** 'Are you *quite* sure those fish are fresh, my man?'

**Fishmonger:** 'Fresh, ma'am? Of course they are!' (Turning to his wares) 'Lie still there, lie still, can't you?'

**Diner:** 'What's all this leathery stuff, waiter?'

**Waiter:** 'Fillet of sole, sir.'

**Diner:** 'Well take it away and see if you can't get me a nice tender cut from the upper part of the boot.'

What happens if one does not eat for seven days?

*It makes one weak (week).*

## To Break a Stick Placed on Two Glasses

The stick used for this trick must not be too thick, and both its ends should be tapered off to a point, and as equal in length as possible so that the centre is obvious.

Rest the ends of the stick on the edges of the glasses which of course should be perfectly even in height, so that the stick lies in a horizontal position without any undue slant on either side. If a smart quick blow is then struck upon its centre, proportioned (as near as can be guessed) to its size and the distance the glasses are from each other, it will be broken in two without its supports being damaged.

## Watch It!

Ask your friend to lend you a watch. Examine it and give a guess as to its value; then bet your friend that he will not be able to answer 'My watch' to three questions that you are going to put to him. The one who wins will keep the watch.

Show him the watch and say 'What have I got in my hand?' He, of course, will reply 'My watch'. Next pick up some other object, repeating the same question. If he names the object, he loses the bet, but if he is on his guard and, remembering the stake, he says 'My watch' he must of course win. You therefore, to divert his attention, should observe to him 'You are certain to win the bet, but supposing I lose? What will you give me?' If confident of success, he replies 'My watch' for the third time, then you can say 'Right, you've won. I keep the watch!'

**Thing No. 16**

## HOW TO TELL THE DIFFERENCE BETWEEN CHALK AND CHEESE

If someone hands you a piece of something and when you say 'What is this?' they say 'It's either a piece of chalk or a piece of cheese but I'm not sure which' you will feel very proud if you can tell them what it is.

This is how you do it:

(i) Put the piece of stuff in a mouse-trap. If you trap a mouse it's probably cheese. Mice don't go much on chalk.

(ii) Try writing with it on a black-board. If you can see what you have written it is chalk. If you can smell what you have written it is cheese.

(iii) If you haven't got a mouse-trap or a blackboard, taste the stuff. This sometimes helps.

# Ask Me Another!

What has nothing left but *nose* when it loses an eye?
*Noise.*

What can go up a chimney down, but can't come down a chimney up?
*An umbrella.*

What is the longest table in the world?
*The multiplication table.*

Why is a list of musical composers like a saucepan?
*Because it is incomplete without a Handel.*

Why do cows wear cowbells?
*Because their horns don't work.*

What is the most afflicted part of a house?
*The window. It is usually full of panes, and you must have seen a window blind!*

If Sioux spells su, eye spells i, and sighed spells side, why doesn't siouxeyesighed spell suicide?

# Picture Puns

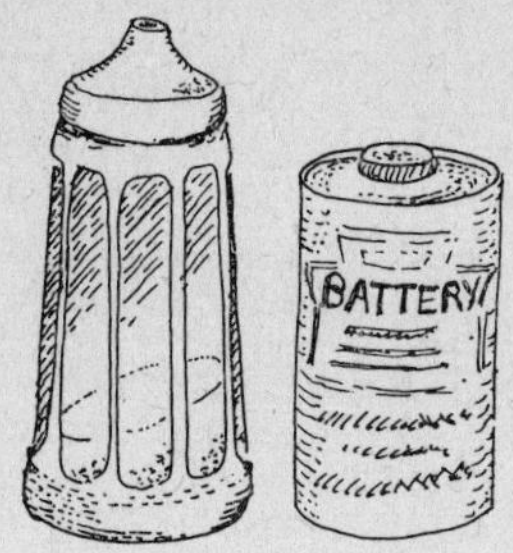


Assault and Battery

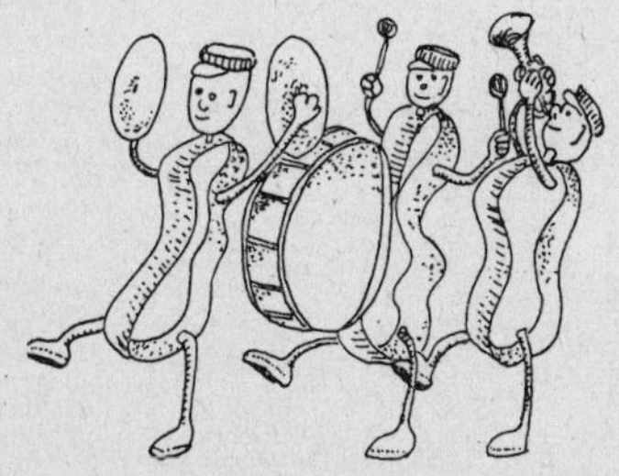

A Rubber Band

Head over Heels

# The Four Friends
## by A. A. Milne

Ernest was an elephant, a great big fellow,
Leonard was a lion with a six-foot tail,
George was a goat, and his beard was yellow,
And James was a very small snail.

Leonard had a stall, and a great big strong one,
Ernest had a manger, and its walls were thick,
George found a pen, but I think it was the wrong one,
And James sat down on a brick.

Ernest started trumpeting, and cracked his manger,
Leonard started roaring, and shivered his stall,
James gave the huffle of a snail in danger
And nobody heard him at all.

Ernest started trumpeting and raised such a rumpus,
Leonard started roaring and trying to kick,
James went a journey with the goat's new compass
And reached the end of his brick.

# The Four Friends

Ernest was an elephant and very well-intentioned,
  Leonard was a lion with a brave new tail,
George was a goat, as I think I have mentioned,
    But James was only a snail.

## A Good Catch

The following is a good catch to try on your friends. Lay a wager with a friend that to three observations you will put to him, he will not be able to reply 'A bottle of wine'. You begin with some commonplace remark such as 'We have had a fine day today' or any other similar remark. He will answer of course 'A bottle of wine'. You then make another remark of the same kind as 'I hope we shall have as fine or finer tomorrow' to which he will reply as before 'A bottle of wine'. The catch comes now. You must say very positively, 'Ah! I've caught you out. You have lost your wager'; and he will say if he is not aware of the trick, 'Why, how do you work that out?' forgetting that though a strange one, it is the third remark that you have made.

## The Balanced Stick

Get a piece of wood 6″ in length and about ½″ thick and near one end of it stick in the blades of two pen-knives, in such a manner that one of them inclines to one side and the second to the other. If the other end of the piece of wood is then placed on the tip of the forefinger, it will keep itself perfectly upright without falling, and even if it is inclined to one side, it will instantly regain its position, because it is kept in equipoise by the two knives.

Thing No. 17

## HOW TO DO THUMB-NAIL SKETCHES

Do them like this:

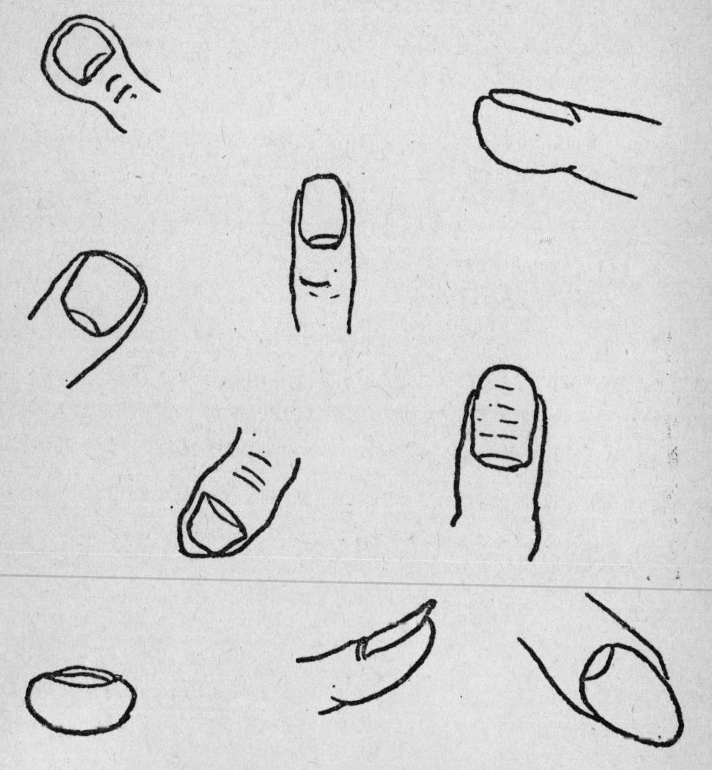

# Nasty Jokes

Dracula lives in the tallest building in America.

*The Vampire State Building.*

We have great pleasure in releasing Dracula's fan(g) club. For details, send your name, address and blood group.

Yesterday a man drowned himself in a cesspool. The coroner gave a verdict of sewercide (suicide).

A medical examiner once asked a candidate in an examination what would be the first thing he would do if a man were blown up by gunpowder. 'Wait till he came down,' replied the young medical student.

Yesterday two ladies went for a tramp in the park. He is now recovering in hospital.

'Mummy, mummy, dad's going out.'

'Well pour some more paraffin on him, dear.'

'Excuse me, sir, there's a man outside with a wooden leg, called Smith.'

'Oh yes? What's his other leg called?'

What's brown and slimy, lives on the sea bed and attacks all the other fish?

*Jack the Kipper!*

# Find the Country

Unjumble these words and you will find a list of countries.

AMBOLICO

CLONSTAD

CRAFEN

ERECEG

LARISE

HANDILAT

KRYUET

PYTEG

USATIRA

VILABIO

LAYTI

ARUNUMI

ATLASURIA

CORCOMO

DELCINA

GAULBRIA

GLIBEUM

LIONOGMA

NESDEW

PLATURGO

RAKMEND

GALENND

# In the Garden

Can you work out what plants are in the garden from the following:

For example, a timid animal and a jingling instrument, hare, bell, harebell.

A pretence and a huge stone.

An emblem of purity and a globule of moisture.

A colour and something one rings.

A cunning animal and an article of clothing.

An affectionate request.

A large city and that which goes before a fall.

A learned man.

A partition and a bloom.

# 'Allo, 'Allo, 'Allo!

**Jim** (boastfully): 'The last man I hit was collected in bits afterwards.'

**Joe** (not to be outdone): 'The last man I hit in this country got fined in Paris.'

**Jim** (suspiciously): 'What for?'

**Joe** (matter-of-factly): 'Flying without a licence.'

'Why are you in prison, my good fellow?'

'For driving a car too slowly, guv'nor.'

'You mean too quickly, don't you?'

'No, slowly, guv. The owner overtook me.'

A man was arrested and brought to court on a charge of stealing watches. Before passing sentence on him the magistrate said:

'How is it that you manage to take the watches without the owners being any the wiser?'

'My fee for lessons is five pounds, your worship,' replied the offender calmly.

Last night a man was seen walking down the road holding a candle which was said to have been stolen.

I suppose you could call him light fingered.

# A Capital Puzzle

Disguised below are 25 European capitals. What are they?

BUD'S TAPE
E. B. GERALD
HE'S NAT
LOBS IN
OMER
RE: BEN
RUE GAP
WAS RAW
ALF BEST
CHAS TRUBE
EVA INN
HOLT MOCKS
MAD MASTER
OPEN CHANGE
RIB LEN
SHIN-LIKE
AS RIP
DR DIAM
HER GIN, BUD
IRA ANT
OLD NON
RUBLESSS
SOLO
AFOSI

# Bird-watching

Each bird is made up of letters of the alphabet. Can you name them?

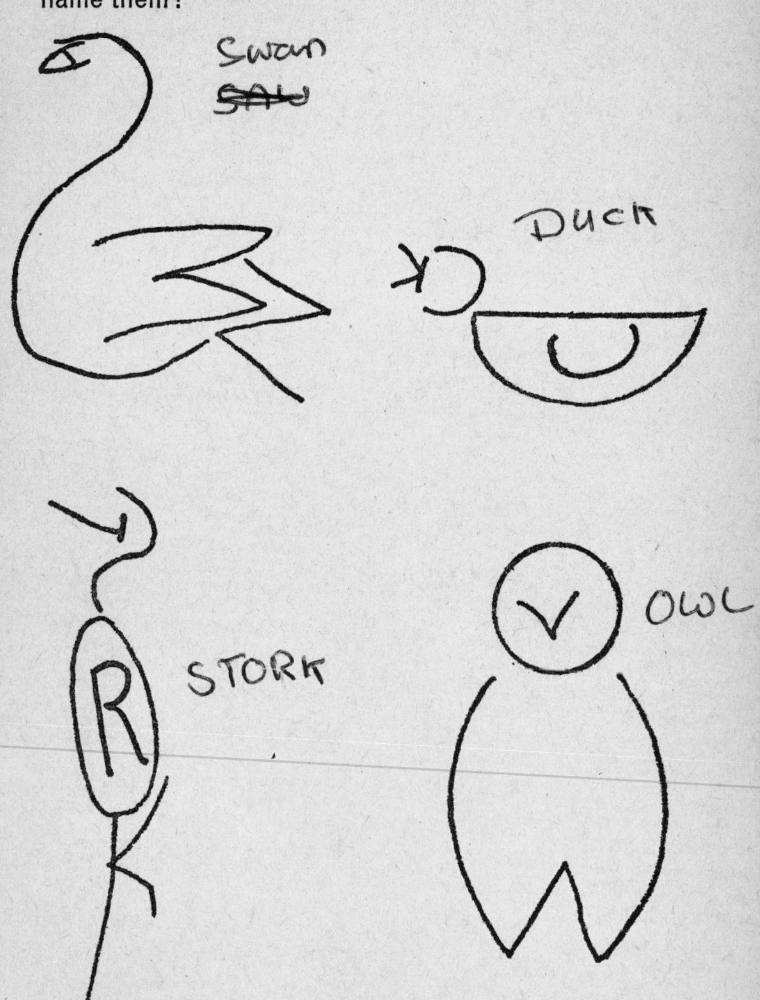

## A Few Last Riddles

Why is a horse that is always ridden and never fed never likely to starve?

*Because he always has a bit in his mouth.*

Why is a bank like a piano?

*Because they both issue forth notes.*

Why is a newspaper never white?

*Because it is always read (red!).*

What has ears and cannot hear?

*Corn.*

In what does one bury a dead clock?

*A winding sheet.*

Why is a cow's tail like a swan's breast?

*Because they both grow down.*

Why is a newspaper boy never cold?

*Because selling papers maintains the circulation.*

Why is a horse cleverer than a mouse?

*Because it can run away when in a trap.*

# At the Circus

By taking the first letter of each object you see, you will discover what is at the circus.

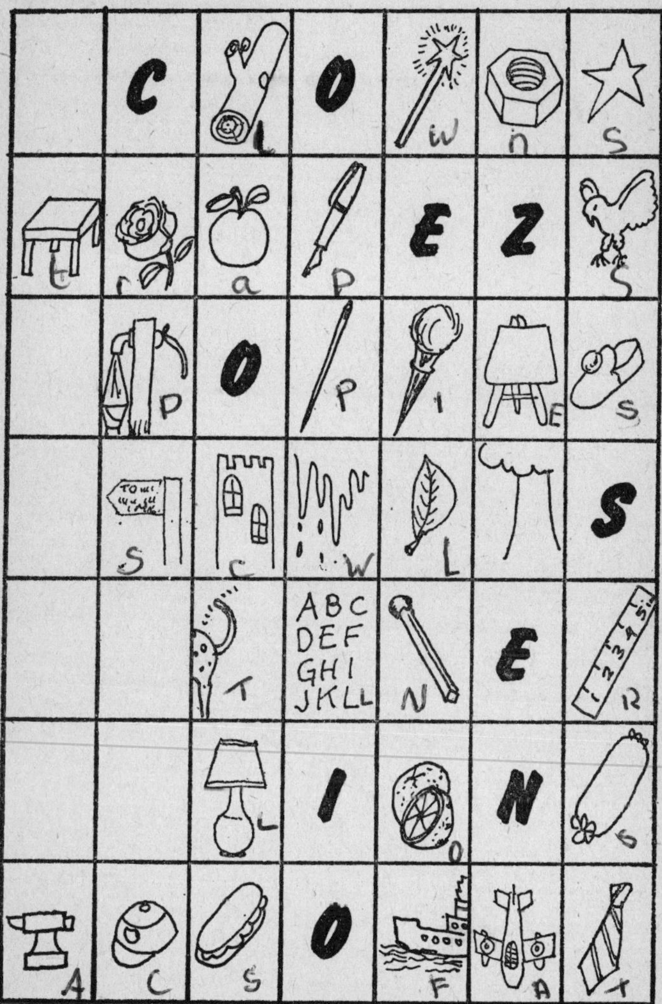

# A Few Last Laughs

Do you know the story about double images?

I'd better not tell you as you might get beside yourself with the excitement.

**Passenger:** 'Conductor, do you stop at the Savoy Hotel?'

**Conductor:** 'What, on my salary?'

Have you heard the story about the record?

Oh, it's been going round for some time.

Going on a ferry boat makes me cross.

Stringing tennis racquets takes a lot of guts.

A very holy vulture could be described as a bird of *pray*!

1st Man: 'What are you thinking about?'

2nd Man: 'A glass of wine.'

1st Man: 'Oh, spiritual meditation.'

Trainer to boxer: 'Are you ready for another fight?'

'Just a bout!'

Recently I saw a bed 20 ft long and 9 ft wide.

Oh, what a lot of bunk.

All musicians live in A Flat.

Did you know that fishermen have to pay 30% of their *net* income? However, they do usually get a *rebait*.

I think gambling is a dicey business.

What is the definition of 'out of pocket'?

*A runaway baby kangaroo.*

If you hear rumours about a runaway saucepan full of green potatoes, just ignore them.

There's nothing in it.

**Beginner:** 'What's the hardest thing about roller skating when you're learning?'

**Instructor:** 'The floor!'

**Shopman:** 'That hat suits you wonderfully, sir.'

**Customer:** 'Yes, but what happens when my ears get tired?'

**Lunatic** (pointing to clock): 'Is that clock right?'

**Warder:** 'Yes.'

**Lunatic:** 'Well, what's it doing in a lunatic asylum then?'

**Joe:** 'Hallo, Pat. Are you off to the North Pole?'

**Pat:** 'No. I'm just going to paint the back door.'

**Joe:** 'But why are you wearing all those clothes?'

**Pat:** 'Because it says on the bottle: "To obtain best results, put on three to four coats." '

**First Man:** What are your hobbies?

**Second Man:** I race pigeons.

**First Man:** Oh, have you ever beaten one?

What does one get if one crosses a sheepdog with a jelly?

*The collie wobbles.*

I used to be a fortune teller but I gave it up. There wasn't any future in it.

Have you heard about the thin mouse?
He had a narrow squeak.

# Answers

Page 11

## Wordladder Puzzle

Hull, hall, hale, hare, bare, bale, ball, bill, bull, dull, duel, Deal.

Page 15

## Up the Garden Path

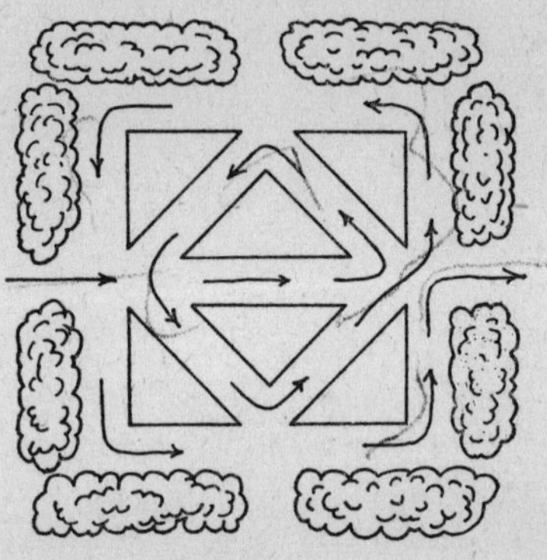

Page 21

## Puzzle Park

Bench, flowers, swings, path, trees, railing, ducks, pond.

Page 32

## Spot the Difference

In the lower picture: 1. the cow has a patch missing 2. the cow has no bell 3. only one crossbar on the gate 4. a small puddle is missing 5. no top left-hand window on the house 6. one chimney pot missing on the left chimney stack 7. a distant bush on the left has disappeared 8. the wall has gone 9. one cloud on the left is missing 10. a tree on the distant right has vanished.

Page 33

## A Noisy Puzzle

Scream, bang, howl, roar, whoop, cluck, wail, clatter, crash, hiss.

## Jumbled Clothing

Blouse, shoes, coat, gloves, scarf, skirt, dress, socks, cardigan, tie.

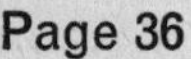
Page 36

## Fun with Matches

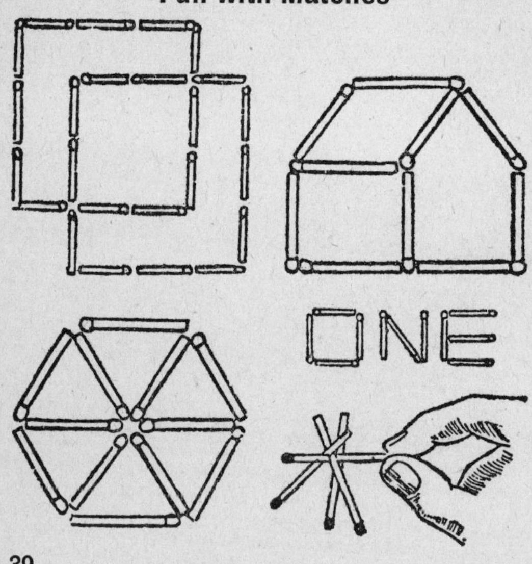


Page 39

## A Fishy Puzzle

Shark, cod, plaice, herring, salmon.

Page 42

## The Puzzled Cat

Cattle, catherine wheel, caterpillar, cataclysm, catch, catechism, catarrh, catacomb, catastrophe, cathedral, category, catalogue, catapult, catgut, caters, cataract, catching, catkins, catmint, Catherine.

Page 51

## Find the Colour

White, red, black, scarlet, blue, green, yellow, brown, grey.

## Find the Creature

Cock, pony, owl, bear, cat, pig, goat, hen, seal, bat.

Page 63

## Ninepence Puzzle

Two coins only, D and F, need be moved in order to obtain 10 rows each consisting of 3 coins.

A B C

D E F

G H I

ABC, AEI, ADH, GHI, GEC, GDB, BFI, HFC, BEH, DEF.

Page 65

## Pair the Words

Cupboard, mattress, carpet, teapot, lampshade, settee, armchair, footstool, eiderdown, toaster.

Tumbler, reel, bill, ball, rule, volume, band, spirit, stone.

Page 73

## Find the Twins

Pictures D and E are the same.

Page 77

## Word Squares

Rim, knight, cold, say, spot, sit, funny, met.

Kitten, dawn, actor, old, rap, apple, nod.

Page 81

## Seaside Picture Puzzle

Sand, starfish, sea, donkeys, gulls, rockpool, icecream, bucket.

Page 88

## Hunt the Animal

Fox, bat, ermine, beaver, jaguar, ass, leopard, giraffe, lion, jackal, hare, hippopotamus, llama, marmot, hedgehog, whale, horse, onyx, elephant, bear, sheep, lemming, mongoose, panther, porcupine, baboon.

Blackboard, pencil, ruler, pictures, desk, book, chalk.

Page 90

## Knitting-needle Puzzle

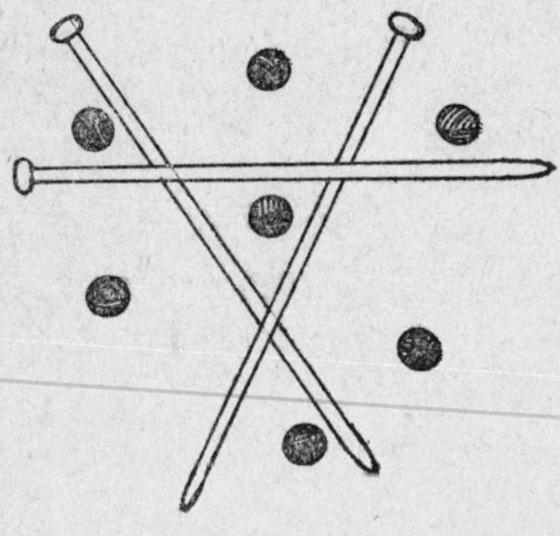

Page 94

## Rabbit Maze

Ian found his way home.

Page 113

## Find the Country

Colombia, Scotland, France, Greece, Israel, Thailand, Turkey, Egypt, Austria, Bolivia, Italy, Rumania, Australia, Morocco, Iceland, Bulgaria, Belgium, Mongolia, Sweden, Portugal, Denmark, England.

Page 114

## In the Garden

Shamrock, snowdrop, bluebell, foxglove, forget-me-not, London pride, sage, wallflower.

Page 116

## A Capital Puzzle

Budapest, Belgrade, Athens, Lisbon, Rome, Berne, Prague, Warsaw, Belfast, Bucharest, Vienna, Stockholm, Amsterdam, Copenhagen, Berlin, Helsinki, Paris, Madrid, Edinburgh, Tirana, London, Brussels, Oslo, Sofia.

Page 117

## Bird-watching

Swan, duck, stork, owl.

Page 119

## At the Circus

Clowns, trapeze, ponies, stilts, tamer, lions, acrobat.

STAY ON

Here are details of other exciting TARGET titles. If you cannot obtain these books from your local bookshop, or newsagent, write to the address below listing the titles you would like and enclosing cheque or postal order—*not* currency—including 7p per book to cover packing and postage; 2–4 books, 5p per copy; 5–8 books, 4p per copy.

TARGET BOOKS,
Universal-Tandem Publishing Co.,
14 Gloucester Road,
London SW7 4RD

---

**AGATON SAX AND THE DIAMOND THIEVES** 25p
**Nils-Olof Franzen**
0 426 10196 0 **Target Humour**
In which AGATON SAX, world famous newspaper-owner and amateur detective, pits his brilliant brain and iron nerve against the tough, unpleasant and horribly clever Octopus P. Scott in a bid to recover the priceless Koh-mih-Nor diamond . . . and Inspector Lispington of Scotland Yard gets a bucketful of cold porridge over his head! *Illustrated.*